T0145555

Living Without Strain

Living Without Strain

The Inner Meaning of The Book of Job

Joseph Murphy
Ph.D., D.D.

MEDIA

Published 2019 by Gildan Media LLC
aka G&D Media
www.GandDmedia.com

Design by Meghan Day Healey of Story Horse, LLC

Library of Congress Cataloging-in-Publication Data is available upon
request

ISBN: 978-1-7225-0130-3

10   9   8   7   6   5   4   3   2   1

Contents

Introduction
Living Without Strain

The Book of Job is one of the most important, significant, and profound books of the Bible. It has been the subject of theological and philosophical debate for many centuries. The main theme of the book deals with human suffering, setting forth the story of a just and upright man who apparently through no fault of his own meets with all kinds of dire misfortune and calamities, and finally recoups all his losses and experiences happiness, prosperity, and peace of mind. The sublimity, spiritual insight, imagery, symbolic beauty, and excellence of expression make it an ever recurrent inspiration. Its depth of feeling and contemplative content touches the heart strings and plays upon them the eternal song of triumph, victory, and the power to overcome all obstacles.

The great truths embodied in the book of Job are indeed a sanctuary to which all may turn for guidance and light on their problems, for it is a sanctuary built out of the treasure house of the Light of the One Who Forever Is. It opens the door to faith and understanding. It embodies the Great Law of Life.

The book consists of five parts.

1. The prologue, written like the epilogue in prose (chapter 1).
2. The colloquies of Job and his friends (chapters 3–31).
3. The speeches of Elihu (chapters 32–37).
4. The speeches of Jehovah out of the storm with brief answers by Job (chapters 38–42).
5. The epilogue (chapters 42–7–17).

Two literary styles are represented in the book of Job—narrative prose and didactic poetry; both however, are exquisitely presented and artistically executed. The contents of the book of Job are essentially a profound psychological inquiry into the mystery of existence. Scholars do not know who wrote the book of Job, but include it in the group of books of wisdom, of which, it is doubtless one of the greatest. The whole drama is of legendary origin, but it is essentially the story of all men. Spiritually speaking you are Job yourself as you come out of the fog and are regenerated by an Interior Light and begin to sense that God is pushing through you into open manifestation emerging out of misery and suffering into the Beatific Vision!

1

Comments on Chapter 1, The Book of Job

(1) *There was a man in the land of Uz, whose name was Job; and that man was perfect and upright, and one that feared God, and eschewed evil. (2) And there were born unto him seven sons and three daughters. (3) His substance also was seven thousand sheep, and three thousand camels, and five hundred yoke of oxen, and five hundred she asses, and a very great household; so that this man was the greatest of all the men of the east. (4) And his sons went and feasted in their houses, every one his day; and sent and called for their three sisters to eat and to drink with them. (5) And it was so, when the days of their feasting were gone about, that Job sent and sanctified them, and rose up early in the morning, and offered burnt offerings according to the number of them all: for Job said, It may be that*

my sons have sinned, and cursed God in their hearts. Thus did Job continually. (6) Now there was a day when the sons of God came to present themselves before the Lord, and Satan came also among them.

The first verse means that we are all born into this world which is called Uz, i.e., the conditioned state. We are born into all that our environment represents and are conditioned by parental influence, environmental surroundings, plus the influence of the race mind. Every individual is really a group of beliefs, opinions, and concepts which clothe the real Being. The word *man* in Sanskrit means "the measurer". Hence, man is a mind that measures all things. You are in the land of Uz, a conditioned world or state of limitation, bondage, and restriction until you awaken to your inner potentialities. Every child born in the world is the Infinite One assuming the form of that child.

You come into this world for the joy of self-discovery. If your inner powers functioned automatically, you would never be able to discover yourself. It is possible for you to use the life forces both positively and negatively otherwise you would never be able to grow, expand, or deduce a law from them. All of us remain under the bondage of our hereditary concepts, early theological training, and doctrinal beliefs until we learn about the creative capacity of our own mind to alter conditions and bring to fruition the cherished desires of our heart. On the heels of the discovery of the mental and spiritual laws of life, you throw off the yoke of bondage and cease to submit to the hypnotic spell of the world of opinions and false beliefs.

In order to awaken to your higher powers, you must cease being a baby and break this infantile identification with the fleshly self. You must prove that you are not just flesh but merely functioning in the flesh. All your thoughts, feelings, emotions, imaginings, and dreams are invisible, and I cannot see your mind or spirit, neither can I perceive your faith, hope, trust, love, joy, affection, pondering, desires, longings, aversions, likes, or dislikes—all are themselves invisible. They constitute you! You are much more than your body, the latter is simply your mind condensed or Spirit in manifestation.

In verse one it says, "That man was perfect and upright, and one that feared God, and eschewed evil." The average child born in love is free from fear, sickness, and distortions of any kind. *God hath not given us the spirit of fear; but of power, and of love, and of a sound mind.* When young you had wonderful health, you were bubbling over with energy, joy, enthusiasm, and vitality. You knew nothing about war, crime, sickness, disease, man's inhumanity to man, or of the conflicting theologies, or the maze of religious dogmas, and the superstitious fears of the multitude. In the cradle you were innocent, and in your imagination you probably played with angels.

Verse two. Your *seven sons* are seeing, feeling, tasting, hearing, smelling, conceiving, and reproduction. In early life we naturally use these faculties positively, actively, mostly in good experiences. When these faculties become passive, receptive, and subject to external negative influences and false concepts, they become symbolized as seven daughters. (*Moses meets seven daughters in Egypt.* EXOD. 2:16).

The three daughters mentioned in verse two are in all of us. It is the trinity or the creative capacity in all of us which enables us to bring forth our ideas as form, experience, and events. There were Trinitarian doctrines long before Christianity. The doctrine of the trinity or triune God was taught in ancient India, Babylon, China, Egypt, and all the countries of the northern latitudes. In China the trinity was symbolized by the father, mother, and child, or idea, feeling, and manifestation. It takes two things to produce a third. A clear and definite thought plus a warmth of feeling will bring about a fusion resulting in a third expression which is the answer to your prayer.

The ancient Hebrews wrote under a system of numerical symbolism and if we add seven plus three we get ten, and the latter symbolizes God in action in our lives. 0 is the symbol of the female and 1 is the symbol of the male. In simple language the book of Job is telling us about the interaction of the male and female principle within ourselves, or the interplay of our conscious and subconscious mind. Each letter in the Hebrew language is assigned a numerical value, and if we add up the Hebrew letters of the name Job we get ten or the complete man.

$$\begin{array}{ccc} J & O & B \\ 1 & 7 & 2 \end{array} = 10$$

The subconscious mind might be called our wife, and the conscious reasoning mind the husband. Our body is simply the instrument which our mind uses. Our conscious and subconscious mind* are always interacting and from their union come forth all our experiences, conditions, and circumstances whether positive or negative. The harmonious and peaceful interrelationship of these two phases of our mind produce health, success, and joyous living. The male element in you may be considered as your thought, idea, plan, image, or purpose; the female in you is emotion, feeling, enthusiasm, faith, and receptivity. The male

---

* See *Miracles of Your Mind*, Chapter One.

and female principle exists in all of us, and this is the reason you are creative and have the power to bring forth out of the depth of yourself that which you emotionalize and feel as true within yourself. When your idea and feeling unite and become one, that one is God in action, for your Divine Creative Power is now made manifest as guidance, healing, or true place in life.

There is one Creative Power in all the world, and that Creative Power is God. When you discover the power of your thought and feeling, you have discovered the Power of God in yourself. All the trials, tribulations, sufferings, and misery of our neurotic age are due to the inharmonious interaction between the conscious and the subconscious of men and women everywhere. When you enthrone the proper concepts and ideas in the conscious mind, these will generate the right feeling; then the mind and the heart or the male and female principle are working together in concord and unity. If our thoughts are negative, our feelings will also be negative because emotions follow thought. If your thoughts are fearful, vicious, or destructive, powerful negative emotions are generated and lodged in the inner recesses of your subconscious mind. These negative emotions get snarled up and form complexes, and inasmuch as emotions must have an outlet, it is obvious that such emotions will erupt in disease and destructive mental aberrations of all kinds.

Verses five, six, and seven. The first thing you should do when you arise in the morning is to commune with God and invoke His blessings and inspirations on all your undertakings for the day. Put God first in your life. The *sons* spoken of in verse five are ideas, thoughts, plans, images of the mind; these must be sanctified by seeing to it that all your thoughts, ideas, and purposes conform to the divine standard of whatsoever things are true, noble, lovely, and of good report. Do not condemn yourself if your *sons* (thoughts) are negative, or for getting out of sorts at times, but fill your mind with the eternal truths of God, and become recharged spiritually. That depressed feeling may be due to the influence of the great psychic sea in which we all live; the moods of fear, hate, jealousy, intrigue, and doubt are in the race mind, and in an unguarded moment these negative vibrations may enter our mind and we feel gloomy, despondent, and sad. The negative mental and emotional atmosphere of a place could penetrate your mind and dampen your spirits, inhibit your enthusiasm, and generally put the brakes on your ardor. When this happens, go within, and with the sword of truth and spiritual understanding cast out the dark and false thoughts and affirm your trust, faith, and confidence in the love and goodness of God.

Verse six. *Sons of God* represent good, constructive ideas which come out of the depths of yourself as inspiration and holy desires. *Satan* means opposition or your enemy.

You are told the enemies are of your own household or mind. You must look within for the evil one or negative thought in your mind. The supposed dialogue taking place between the *Lord* and *Satan* as mentioned in verse seven merely means the argumentative process or spiritual reasoning taking place in your own mind whereby you cast out the opposing thoughts in your mind and accept your ideal.

The *Lord* is your dominant desire, the idea which is uppermost in your mind; it might be the desire for health, true place, or guidance you are seeking. You know that your thoughts come as pairs. You desire health, which is an affirmative and positive concept, but immediately there arises an opposing or negative concept to challenge it. You desire wealth, and an opposing thought comes into your mind reminding you perhaps that you are broke, and that all is lost, and that there is no way out. There is no devil going to and fro on the earth planting negative thoughts in our mind, but for every yea there is a nay. The so-called devil is the belief in a suppositional opposing power to God which creates a conflict in the mind causing a double-minded or unstable state. The enemy, destroyer, adversary, or devil is a belief in lack, limitation, failure, sickness, and intimations of impotency and inadequacy which you allow to creep into the mind. The devils* which bedevil you are your hates, jealousies, fears, anxieties, and tensions.

The word *Satan* means to err, to slip, to turn away from God and the Truth, and from the belief in One Power. *Satan* also means the race mind, the world mind which impinges on all of us, casting its hypnotic spell of lack, limitation, and misery. *Satan* is nothing trying to be something. You reject *Satan* when you completely rout out of your mind incisively and decisively the thought that you cannot achieve or accomplish. You must positively refuse to admit fears and doubts into your mind because these are lies about Omnipotence or God which are within you. The thought of failure is an illusion of power; it has no power.

(7) *And the Lord said unto Satan, Whence comest thou? Then Satan answered the Lord, and said, From going to and fro in the earth, and from walking up and down in it.*

Verse seven tells you that *Satan* is a myth for there is no such being going to and fro in the earth, and walking up and down in it. An old acquaintance of mine placed implicit trust in his partner; the latter

---

* See *How to Use Your Healing Power*, Chapter One.

proved to be deceitful and betrayed his trust in him, and absconded with all the money in the bank. My friend was strongly tempted to resent and hate him and wish for him all manner of evil. He said to me, "I took that man in, befriended him, gave him fifty percent interest in the business without any financial consideration." He began to grow very bitter until I pointed out the dangers and the disastrous results which would follow his destructive passion of anger, hatred, and animosity. He realized suddenly and instantaneously that the enemy (devil) was not another person, but a hateful thought of his own choosing which would ultimately destroy him physically and mentally. He completely rejected the temptation to think viciously and destructively of the other, and he began to invoke the influx of the Holy Spirit into his life, claiming God's Guidance and His Love regularly and systematically. He changed his thoughts to conform to Divine Law of Love and Good Will. He blessed and prayed for his ex-partner who disappeared into some foreign country, and was never found. Every time he thought of him he said, "God be with you." Finally, he was able to meet his former partner in his mind and actually emanate a wave of God's peace to him. The acid test of forgiveness is to ask yourself, "How do I meet John or Mary in my Mind?" Do you radiate good will and God's blessing to them? If a wave of peace or inner benediction from your heart wells up, you can rest assured you have cleansed both your conscious and subconscious mind.

(8) *And the Lord said unto Satan, Hast thou considered my servant Job, that there is none like him in the earth, a perfect and an upright man, one that feareth God, and escheweth evil?* (9) *Then Satan answered the Lord, and said, Doth Job fear God for nought?* (10) *Hast not thou made an hedge about him, and about his house, and about all that he hath on every side? thou hast blessed the work of his hands, and his substance is increased in the land.* (11) *But put forth thine hand now, and touch all that he hath, and he will curse thee to thy face.*

Here *Satan* is depicted as answering the Lord, "O yes, Job is true to you (Lord) so long as all goes well with his fortune. Let something bad turn up and he will curse thee to thy face." The cry of Job is the cry of every man who walks the earth. That which I am and that which I want to be are always quarrelling in my mind. Through spiritual awareness, man can solve the problem.

There is the inner desire to grow, expand, achieve, accomplish, and move forward. There is the Divine or Cosmic urge in all of us to release our God given powers and attributes and go forth conquering and to conquer. However, conditions, circumstances, opinions of others, and fear thoughts in our mind impede our progress. The material facts seem to preclude and obstruct the realization of our desires.

Man wants a healing, but he is told he is incurable, that the condition is hopeless; he listens to opinions of friends and becomes unduly impressed by the formidable barriers erected by them, and finally he succumbs to hopelessness and despair. This is the perennial quarrel between the lower and the higher self of man, between you and your ideal or desire, the material facts of life, the race mind beliefs challenging the spiritual aspirations, urges, and ideals within you.

Your personal lord is your dominant idea or desire, or that which commands your attention. Whatever interests you most may be considered your lord because it rules your thoughts and emotions. If you are sick, you detach your attention from all your aches, symptoms, and pains and begin to concentrate on the Healing Presence within, knowing that your whole body is being transformed by His Healing Light, feeling and knowing that as you call upon It you receive an answer which is perfect health and harmony. Focusing your attention on God and His Healing Rays you are present with your lord.

Satan (negative thoughts) challenges you as you pray for a healing—this means fear, doubt, anxiety arises in your mind trying to dissuade you from believing in the power of God. These race mind thoughts and opinions of man will sometimes mock you and laugh at you and say to you, "It's impossible." "It's too late now." "You are too far gone." "It's hopeless." Whenever there is such a quarrel in the mind or whenever you suffer from any limitation, restriction, or sense of bondage, this is Satan or the so-called devil alongside your goal or ambition.

Dr. Phineas Parkhurst Quimby, the antecessor and father of mental and spiritual healing in this country, used the argumentative method of healing in many of his cases which is so popular today. Quimby would say to the patient, "Give me your case and I will plead for you before the Great Tribunal, and prove your innocence," and he had remarkable and amazing results. The whole process resolved itself into realizing that the sickness or disease was due to a false idea, distorted pattern, or false direction given the mind which accepted the picture you gave it and brought forth accordingly. Quimby's process was to convince the patient that thoughts are things and that the Spirit within is God. He built up evidence for the truth showing that fear, sickness, disease are not of God, but due to negative thinking, and that these thoughts solidified and became tumorous growths, tuberculosis, etc., in the body. He explained to his patients that their fears were groundless because there is no external power, no power but God. He pointed out to his patients that God cannot be sick, frustrated, or unhappy, that the sickness, problem, or difficulty is called Satan because it denies the true spiritual values necessary for our unfoldment. The negative thought in the mind has no principle behind it, no power in and of itself, nothing to back it up; it is a shadow of the mind; it merely denies the positive values within you.

Quimby taught his patients to give all power to God and His Healing Presence. His method was to contemplate their Divine perfection and redirect their minds according to the Divine archetype of harmony, health, and peace. Remarkable healings followed this process and methodology. You overcome Satan by detaching yourself from the world and sense evidence and being mentally present with the Wisdom and Power of the Almighty.

Let your attention rest in God and His Love remembering wherever your attention is, there the Creative Power of God moves on your behalf. All the power of the Infinite One relative to you and your desire is present and operating at that focal point of attention. This was the secret of Quimby's remarkable healings, and the same process will bring countless blessings in your life.

(15) *And the Sabeans fell upon them, and took them away; yea, they have slain the servants with the edge of*

the sword; and I only am escaped alone to tell thee. (16)
*While he was yet speaking, there came also another,
and said, The fire of God is fallen from heaven, and
hath burned up the sheep, and the servants, and consumed them; and I only am escaped alone to tell thee.*
(17) *While he was yet speaking, there came also another,
and said, The Chaldeans made out three bands, and fell
upon the camels, and have carried them away, yea, and
slain the servants with the edge of the sword; and I only
am escaped to tell thee.*

Where these and other verses in Chapter One
speak of Sabeans, Chaldeans, etc., they represent
thoughts of limitation, intemperance, beliefs in the
power of the stars, bondage to the past, such as karma,
which enter into Job's mind to plague him.

(21) *And said, Naked came I out of my mother's
womb, and naked shall I return thither: the Lord gave,
and the Lord hath taken away; blessed be the name of
the Lord.*

Here we are dealing with the Law of cause and
effect which is impersonal. It will bring forth sickness or health, peace or pain, sorrow or joy, poverty or
abundance, success or failure with the same completeness. *I form the light, and create darkness: I make peace,
and create evil: I the Lord do all these things.* ISAIAH 45:7.

You must realize the interchangeability of *Lord* and
Law. It is not that a God of Love creates a devil or evil.

The answer is that the *Law* (Lord) is the automatic bringer of man's thoughts into manifestation. Think evil, evil follows; think good, good follows. Your mind is like water which takes the shape of any vessel in which it is poured. The vessel is your thought patterns and mental imagery which the Creative Power flows through and brings to pass in your experience. Your deeper mind called the subconscious is the fabricator which weaves the pattern of your thoughts into your experience and conditions. Feed the mind with premises which are true, noble, and Godlike, and you will find the subconscious is your best friend providing that which is beautiful, lovely, and glorious in your outer world.

2

Comments on Chapter 2, The Book of Job

(3) And the Lord said unto Satan, Hast thou considered my servant Job, that there is none like him in the earth, a perfect and an upright man, one that feareth God and escheweth evil? and still he holdeth fast his integrity, although thou movedst me against him, to destroy him without cause. (4) And Satan answered the Lord, and said, Skin for skin, yea, all that a man hath will he give for his life. (5) But put forth thine hand now, and touch his bone and his flesh, and he will curse thee to thy face. (6) And the Lord said unto Satan, Behold, he is in thine hand; but save his life. (7) So went Satan forth from the presence of the Lord, and smote Job with sore boils from the sole of his foot unto his crown. (8) And he took him a potsherd to scrape himself withal; and he sat down among the ashes. (9) Then said his

wife unto him, Dost thou still retain thine integrity? curse God, and die.

The test of your faith and trust in God is how do you react in adversity, catastrophe, tragedy, or death of a loved one? When everything goes wrong, when sickness strikes, how do you respond? This is the time when you should apply your knowledge of the laws of mind by keeping your eyes on the goal, on what you desire. Believe it is yours now because you feel it in your heart. Your desire is as real as your hand, accept it, and you will see it appear on the screen of space. In the backfield, if you fall down you have to get up smiling because you know the next time you play, victory will be yours.

When things are running smoothly and man is waxing rich, he is inclined to relax, take matters easy, and cease to pray. However, when trouble comes, he begins to ask all kinds of questions such as, "Why did this happen to me?" "I was not thinking of this disease at all." "I never heard of it." "I hate no one." "I have done good all my life." "I gave to the poor." "I go to church." etc.

Verses six and seven point out that Job was covered with boils from the sole of his foot unto his crown.

In verse nine Job's wife says to him to curse God and die. Your wife is your feeling, emotion, reaction; man sometimes curses God when his child dies, or when some misfortune comes into his life. What man needs is a clear understanding of the law of his own being which is *it is done unto him as he believes.*

Belief is a thought in the mind. A man may be a regular communicant or attendant at his church, he may observe all the rules, rites, rituals, and ceremonies, and still suffer sickness, tragedies, and all kind of seeming misfortunes. It is the way man thinks, feels, and believes in his heart that matters; in other words, the inner movement of the heart is always made manifest. Thus a man may be a good Buddhist, Moslem, Christian, or Jew, and adhere to the basic tenets of these religions and yet suffer misery, pain, and penury. *As a man thinketh in his heart, so is he.* Your heart is a Chaldean word meaning your subconscious mind— the seat of your feelings and emotions.

I knew a woman who was very good from the world's viewpoint. She went to church regularly, gave liberally to charities, visited hospitals, also gave free lessons in music to poor children in the neighborhood, yet she was crippled with arthritis. She told me that she believed God was punishing her because she had sinned forty years previously. I also discovered she dreaded death because she feared she would be judged and found wanting; she believed in a literal hell. In addition, she secretly hated her daughter-in-law, but gave her lavish presents at Christmas-time and Easter, and went out of her way to show her apparent kindness to her. What she was really doing was a form of subconscious compensation to appease her deep sense of guilt because of her suppressed hatred for her daughter-in-law.

Her external profession of faith in such and such a church is not what the Bible is talking about, it means your real inner attitude, inner feelings, and movements of the mind. Her negative thinking generated destructive emotions, and these negative emotions snarled up in the subconscious must have an outlet, so her destructive emotions came forth as arthritis. Her devotion, allegiance, and loyalty to her particular church or creed was of no avail. *According to your faith is it done unto you*—this is the law mentioned in the Bible.

Faith is a way of thinking, an inner attitude, a feeling, or inner awareness. A man can have faith in failure, success, misfortune, and poverty, and he will express all these states in his life. This is faith in reverse. Faith is what you behold, agree with, and accept in your mind; actually it is a thought in your mind, and thoughts being creative, we create what we think for man is belief expressed. We create what we really believe in our mind and heart. It is what you really believe deep down in your heart that is important, not that to which you merely give formal or intellectual assent.

The healing of the above-mentioned woman took place following a lengthy explanation plus prayer. In the beginning she was obdurate in her refusal to believe in a God of Love, and I wondered at the obtuseness of her brilliant mind. Her whole religious attitude seemed to be tainted with moral obliquity. She admitted that she wanted a healing, but thought that God wanted her to suffer for her sins. I explained to her that thoughts were things and that if she believed that God poured out his wrath upon her, that the Creative Force would respond according to the nature of her thought, and that actually she was punishing herself. Gradually it dawned in her mind that the law of her mind was simply action (thought) and reaction (response to thought) by her subconscious mind. Her good and evil experiences were simply movements of her own mind relative to the life-principle forever whole and perfect in itself. She began to see as Judge Troward, author of *Edinburgh Lectures,* pointed out that God is all there is, and that God is Infinite, and that it is mathematically and scientifically impossible to have two Infinites. If there were two powers one would cancel out the other, and there would be nothing but chaos and constant friction and strife. If there were some power to challenge God, God would not be Supreme or Omnipotent. *Hear, O Israel: The Lord our God is one Lord.* DEUT. 6:4.

She finally agreed that undoubtedly her mental states were projected into her body and external experiences. Her prayer was as follows: "The Healing Intelligence which created me is focused at the exact spot in my mind where the trouble is, and all mental and physical distortion is removed. Divine Love dissolves everything unlike itself, and I am relaxed and at peace. His River of Peace is saturating and permeating my whole being, and I am relaxed and at peace. His River of Peace floods my mind and body, and I feel wonderful. I fully and freely forgive everyone, and I pour out His Love and Blessings on my daughter-in-law and all those around me, and I am free."

She affirmed these truths slowly, quietly, reverently, and lovingly several times a day, and a complete healing followed in about a month's time.

The Bible says, "Except ye repent, ye shall likewise perish." To repent means to change your thoughts according to spiritual standards, to think in a new way. If you do not fill your mind with nourishing, sustaining, wholesome, inspiring ideas, in other words, if you do not do your constructive thinking, the race mind or great psychic sea in which we live will impinge itself in your consciousness, and you will be governed and at the mercy of the race mind. We are all immersed in the one mind, and if the only mental foods you receive are the negative suggestions of radio, newspapers, and neighbors, further modified by the limitations, fears, and troubles of the race mind which impregnate your mind, you succumb to the mass hypnotic spell of the world mind around you, except you assume control and direction of your mental and emotional forces. This is why so-called good people suffer so much misery in their life.

If you are indifferent, careless, indolent, and lazy, and refuse to fill your mind with the truths of God, the negative thoughts, moods, and beliefs which enter into the unguarded mind impregnate the subconscious, and as we sow, we reap. When you are ignorant or unaware of the mental laws, you may attribute your unpleasant experiences to chance, fate, bad luck, karma, or destiny instead of realizing that behind every effect there is a cause. You must realize that the rain falls on the just and the unjust, and the sun shines on good and bad men with equal radiance. God is no respecter of persons. The difference between men is due to their state of consciousness, and their state of consciousness consists of what they think, feel, believe, and give mental consent to. This is why some are sick, others healthy, why some are poor and others rich, some sad and others bubbling over with the joy of life.

To believe in certain rituals, liturgies, creeds, dogmas, traditional concepts, formulations, and opinions of man is not the answer, but it is to believe in a God of love, goodness, and everlasting righteousness. You must believe that the will of God for us is more and more of life, love, truth, beauty, abundance, and wonderful experiences transcending our fondest dreams. This is real belief because you believe in the goodness and love of God which is true faith in the bliss, joy, wholeness, beauty, and perfection of God. Your faith is now in God and in all things good, and all things work together for good to them that love God. You are now of the true faith because you believe in the Truth about God, and you live in the joy of the expectancy of the best—only the best shall come to you.

(11) *Now when Job's three friends heard of all this evil that was come upon him, they came every one from his own place; Eliphaz the Temanite, and Bildad the Shuhite, and Zophar the Naamathite: for they had made an appointment together to come to mourn with him and to comfort him.*

These three friends represent tradition, doctrine, and dogma when undisciplined and running rampant. The undisciplined, untutored, and unregenerate mind of man splits up and becomes disorganized and completely confused under the dominance of the three so-called friends whose real names are fear, ignorance, and superstition. Job is really being tormented by his own split personality which reflects the opinions of the world rather than the truth which makes you free.

You must become reintegrated with faith and confidence in the God-Presence within, letting the spirit of wholeness, beauty, and perfection flow through you in transcendent loveliness, transforming your mind and body into God's perfect pattern on the mount. The mind must no longer be permitted to set up strange doctrines based on false theories and false gods, such as, the dichotomy of spirit and matter, flesh and spirit, God and a devil, etc. Mental invasions and intrusions of fear propaganda, sickness, disease, and the fears of the world must be met and disarmed by the awareness of the Presence of God in you—the only Cause and the only Power. You take your instructions and orders from Divine Intelligence rather than from the world and its false beliefs.

Begin now to thing, speak, and act from the standpoint of God's Love and Wisdom within, rather than from the superimposed edifice of fear, doubt, and worry. In this way you will begin your trek back to God in the midst of you which is mighty to heal.

3

Comments on Chapter 3, The Book of Job

(1) After this opened Job his mouth, and cursed his day. (2) And Job spake, and said, (3) Let the day perish wherein I was born, and the night in which it was said, There is a man child conceived. (11) Why died I not from the womb? why did I not give up the ghost when I came out of the belly? (12) Why did the knees prevent me? or why the breasts that I should suck? (13) For now should I have lain still and been quiet, I should have slept: then had I been at rest.

One of the purposes of the Book of Job is to explain the different opinions which people have of God. Here Job in his suffering regrets that he was born and wishes he were dead. Chapters three to thirty-two are all about the quarrel which goes on in us as we come to grips with the world beliefs and opinions (Satan); apparently whatever evils and misfortunes befell Job as regards his property, family, and health were all caused by this adversary called Satan. His misfortunes are enumerated in the order as they rank in the average man's estimation. It is customary for men to extol and sing praises to God for His benevolence and blessings when they are prospering and healthy, but when troubles come as described by Job, it is the reverse, murmuring and complaining of injustice; oftentimes execrations and maledictions pour forth from their mouths.

Satan is derived from the same root as seteh which means, "turn away"; it implies the notion of turning away or detaching your attention from a thief; fear thoughts if entertained will tend to turn you away from your abiding faith in God and all things good. If you visit a sick friend and the thought of catching that disease comes to your mind, you must supplant it immediately with the belief in perfect health, for God cannot be sick, and what is true of God is the real truth about you. If you let the picture of the other's ailment dwell in your mind, you are being tempted to engage your mind on an image of sickness. The same idea is contained in the passage, *For the imagination of man's heart is evil from his youth.* GEN. 8:21.

Our thoughts come in pairs, such as health and sickness, wealth and poverty, peace and pain, love and hate. In ancient writings these are referred to as the two angels, or the good and evil inclinations in all people. The negative thought, the evil inclination, the adversary, and the angel of death mentioned in the Bible are identical in meaning. Every person is accompanied by two angels, one being on his right side, one on his left; this is like saying that every desire or wish you have brings with it a negative or opposing thought. For example, you are called on to meet the mortgage and you haven't the money; the desire for God's wealth is real and natural for you, but the negative factor arises in your mind reminding you of your limitation and difficulties. When you are in a quandary, perplexed, and confused, the negative thought is in your mind together with your positive desire. In prayer you hold up the fearful anxious thoughts to the Light, realizing that these negative thoughts are a conglomeration of sinister shadows and that a shadow has no power. You convince yourself that there is but One Power, and because it is omnipotent, it cannot have any antagonists, opposition, or challenger. Your mind then begins to move as a unity, and you ascribe all power to God, and He who gave you the desire will also reveal to you how to bring it to pass in Divine Order.

Judge Troward, in his writings on mental science, points out that your desire has its own mathematics and mechanics with it, and as you sustain it with faith, your desire will come to pass in the right time and in the right way. You bring suffering on yourself by your own wrong thinking, by misapplication and misinterpretation of universal laws. When we fail to pray aright and give attention to the eternal spiritual values of life, pain, misery, and suffering come to remind us of our negligence, indifference, apathy, or slothfulness. Our limitations, problems, and difficulties cause us to seek answers, and in this way we discover the Divinity within.

If the cross word puzzle were all made out for you and all you had to do was to copy the answers, you would soon get bored and jaded. The thrill, the joy, the satisfaction comes in solving the puzzle in the same way as an engineer rejoices when he has successfully spanned the chasm which he was told was impossible. His joy was in overcoming the problem. The Book of Job is really a universally acclaimed classic because it portrays (like the Hindu *Bhagavad-Gita*) the battle which goes on continually in the field of your consciousness (visible and invisible). It is really your story helping you to get an objective view of yourself.

Job has lost the guidance of God and Divine Wisdom which automatically protected him in his youth.

(16) *Or as an hidden untimely birth I had not been; as infants which never saw light.* (17) *There the wicked cease from troubling; and there the weary be at rest.*

Job's friends are tradition, dogma, doctrine (customs, religion, and opinions), and in his mind they concur that he is a sinner because he is nearly dead and fit but to be buried. These arguments take place in the mind of Job in his search for God and His Truth. The questions and answers are repeated, mixed up, and interrupted by Job's description of his acute pain and troubles which had come upon him in spite of his righteousness, charity, and good acts. The answers which Job receives from his friends are exhortations to patience, and speeches intended to make him forget his grief.

4

Comments on Chapter 4, The Book of Job

(1) Then Eliphaz the Temanite answered and said, (2) If we assay to commune with thee, wilt thou be grieved? but who can withhold himself from speaking? (8) Even as I have seen, they that plow iniquity, and sow wickedness, reap the same. (9) By the blast of God they perish, and by the breath of his nostrils are they consumed.

Eliphaz typifies the intellect and approach to God with its complete line of theories about God, existence, and justice. Job is really tormented and persecuted by his own fears, doubts, self-criticism, and self-condemnation which reflect the opinions of the world rather than the awareness of the Truth which would set him free.

(14) *Fear came upon me, and trembling, which made all my bones to shake.* (15) *Then a spirit passed before my face; the hair of my flesh stood up;* (16) *It stood still, but I could not discern the form thereof: an image was before mine eyes, there was silence, and I heard a voice, saying,* (17) *Shall mortal man be more just than God? shall a man be more pure than his maker?*

Here Job is asleep to wisdom and cries out for an explanation. He fears until the hair of his flesh stood up. Creed and dogma represented by Eliphaz are of no avail to Job in his suffering; he gets no answer. Eliphaz tells him that they that sow wickedness reap the same. Such a statement is no comfort to a man whose body is wracked with pain. Moral precepts are not enough.

The plot of Job is a test to see whether man really knows God, or when adversity and tragedy strike he will denounce and reject the concept of God. This is really what the story is all about. A man may be very religious from a worldly standpoint; he may be a good Catholic, Protestant, Jew, or Buddhist, or any other religious faith, he may follow all the rites, rituals, ceremonies and be a regular attendant or communicant of the particular church, yet he may suffer the tortures of the damned. I have just returned from a visit to a hospital to see a man who is crippled and suffering great pain. He told me how he taught Sunday school for forty years, how he worked for the Boy Scouts, helped the crippled children, and performed countless generous and magnanimous deeds, yet he had a so-called incurable disease, lost vision of one eye, and his hearing was almost gone. He said to me, "Why am I suffering? I am a good Christian, and have done a lot of good. Why is God punishing me?"

He cried out like Job and asked the same questions. In talking to him for over an hour, I discerned he had hated a business associate for thirty years. He was warped by a vengeful and malicious emotion and obdurate in his refusal to forgive; he invoked imprecations and maledictions on this associate. This state of consciousness was his real religion; your thoughts, feelings, and inner beliefs represent your religion or relationship to life which is always perfect and whole. It was done unto him as he believed.

The law of life is the law of belief, and belief is a thought in your mind. His thoughts of the other man were hateful, spiteful, and vengeful, which generated a destructive emotion in his subconscious mind where it was snarled up, and inasmuch as these emotions of hate, jealousy, and vengeance must have an outlet, they came forth in him as bodily disease. The reason why some people are sick and others healthy is due to the difference in their belief. It is your real inner subjective beliefs which are made manifest. Your real and true religion was explained thousands of years ago. *As a man thinketh in his heart, so is he.* An ancient sage said, "When you name it, you cannot find it, and when you find it, you cannot name it."

How can you place a sectarian label on peace, love, joy, wisdom, understanding, patience, kindness, good will, justice, illumination, divine wisdom and compassion? These are qualities, attributes, and potencies of God and they belong to all men. As you begin to express these qualities of God, you are beginning to build the Kingdom of God on earth. Your external attachment to a particular church, group, or religious organization is not of primary importance; the acid test of your religious faith is the way you feel in your heart. If you are friendly with God, if you love the Truth, if you are loyal to God, if you radiate love and good will to others, if you are happy, joyous, and free, and living in the joyous expectancy of the best, you have a marvelous religion regardless of whether you belong to any church or not. *Go thy way, and as thou has believed, so be it done unto thee.*

What will you believe in? You are told to believe that God is Wonderful, the Mighty God, the Everlasting Father, the Counsellor, and the Prince of Peace; therefore you should begin now to believe that God is your loving Father who watches over you, guides, and directs you, sustains and strengthens you, and that His Love fills your soul. Believe that God is a lamp unto your feet and a Light on your path. Believe in the abundant life and that the will of God for you is something transcending your fondest dreams. The Bible is not telling you to believe in creeds, dogmas, traditions, churches, or a certain theology; on the contrary the truths of the Bible existed before any church ever existed or before any man ever walked the earth. The principles underlying radio, television, radar always existed. Moses and Jesus could have used loud speakers and jet planes in their journeys. The eternal verities, the qualities of God and His Law are the same yesterday, today, and forever. God and His Law change not, man is variable and inconstant. God and His Truth are immutable, changeless, timeless, and ageless. Love, Wisdom, Joy, Beauty, Intelligence, Harmony, Divine Order were never born and will never die. The only true religion in the world is to express the truth about God.

What is true of God is true of man for man and God are one. There is only One Being and man is that Being in expression; the qualities and powers of the Father must be in the son, therefore we should claim our sonship now and release the imprisoned splendor that is within. When someone asks you what is your faith, you should reply that you have faith in the infinite goodness of God, in His embracing Love, in Eternal Life, in perfect health, in God's abundance and unfailing supply. Announce that you have implicit faith in the law of God which always responds to the nature of your thought (your request). You have faith that when you ask for bread, God your loving Father will not give you a stone; you know in your heart that when you ask for a fish, He, your Loving and Beneficent Father will not give you a serpent. You have faith in the good for God is infinitely good and perfect. Let this answer suffice.

I talked along the above lines to the aforementioned sick man, and he responded after a rather lengthy discussion. He entered into the spirit of forgiveness and invoked the blessings of the Almighty on his partner and on himself. For about ten minutes he called out loud affirming, "God's Love fills my mind and body." A remarkable mental and physical change has taken place, and I feel sure as I write this that he will experience God's grace and a perfect healing. Love in the heart carries love to all the cells of the body, and then only God dwells therein, and God is Love. Love within, Love without, Peace within, Peace without.

In verse sixteen Eliphaz, lost in form, ritual, and doctrinal concepts of God vaguely senses God as a dispenser of justice, he beholds an image surrounded by a silence from which emanated a voice which prates without wisdom.

5

Comments on Chapter 5, The Book of Job

(7) Yet man is born unto trouble, as the sparks fly upward. (17) Behold, happy is the man whom God correcteth: therefore despise not thou the chastening of the Almighty:

Eliphaz sees but does not understand as he simply deals with externals and materialistic concepts of causation. He does not understand that all suffering is due to reaction of the subconscious mind to our negative thinking or our failure to think constructively, because if we fail to give harmonious and constructive patterns to our deeper mind, and if we neglect to feed our mind with premises which are true by dwelling on whatsoever things are lovely and of good report, we must needs suffer accordingly. If we do not choose and select our thoughts, ideas, and mental images, the race mind, or the newspapers, or other people will control our thinking and our moods.

(22) *At destruction and famine thou shalt laugh: neither shalt thou be afraid of the beasts of the earth.* (27) *Lo this, we have searched it, so it is; hear it, and know thou it for thy good.*

Choose your own thoughts and your own emotions, or the world with its vainglory, fears, doubts, hates and jealousies, intrigue and confusion will push you around, and you will be a slave and not a master. Ignorance rules where Wisdom is absent, and ignorance is Satan which is the despoiler of your soul. Idle and futile is the voice of fear when it clamors for peace. Love responds to the call of love for *deep calleth unto deep.*

6

Comments on Chapter 6, The Book of Job

(1) But Job answered and said, (2) Oh that my grief were thoroughly weighed, and my calamity laid in the balances together! (6) Can that which is unsavoury be eaten without salt? or is there any taste in the white of an egg?

Job's reply is that Eliphaz is just preaching, he is saying in effect that he knows he is going in the wrong direction but he wants to be shown wherein he is wrong, and he lets it be known in a rather contentious and churlish fashion by saying to Eliphaz that his arguments are as insipid as the white of an egg.

(11) What is my strength, that I should hope? and what is mine end, that I should prolong my life? (12) Is my strength the strength of stones? or is my flesh of brass?

(13) *Is not my help in me? and is wisdom driven quite from me?*

Here Job strikes spiritual fire when he says, "Is not my help in me? and is wisdom driven from me?" It is beginning to dawn in his mind that God is within him. Eliphaz, the traditional concept of an anthropomorphic being, believes in a God in the skies or somewhere outside. Of course, God is everywhere, inside and outside, for Life or God is omnipresent. When I was a boy studying catechism, I was told that an atheist was a man who did not believe in God, but when I asked the whereabouts of God, I was told he was on a throne in heaven and if I were a good boy and did not commit mortal sins, I might possibly go there and see Him some day and play the harp. I must have been an atheist when I was very young, because I did not believe in the answer, but I knew that some day I would get answers. I discovered that the teacher of catechism did not seem to know anything worth while, that no one knew anything. They had words without meaning, prayers without understanding, religion without science, beliefs without knowledge, faith without feeling, God with a devil, and heaven with hell.

In verse twenty-four Job pleads, *Teach me, and I will hold my tongue and cause me to understand wherein I have erred.*

You ask for bread, and the world gives you a stone in the way of false information based on fear, ignorance, and superstition which are also representative of Job's three friends. You are told the reason you are sick is because you are a miserable sinner, or God is punishing you, or He is testing you, and this explanation makes you feel worse than before. You asked someone why your child died, and he said, "It is God's will." This you found hard to believe and perhaps you cursed God and deserted your church and became an atheist.

I have known cases where children died because parents were careless, indifferent, and unwilling to spend the money to call a physician who would have undoubtedly saved the lives of these children—these same people said it was God's will. To say that death for a child is the will of God is blasphemy. Life cannot wish death. God is Life and Life loves to manifest itself as bliss, harmony, joy, beauty, love, peace, order, and symmetry. The will of God is the nature of God, and His will for us must of necessity be something wonderful, miraculous, glorious, and ecstatic.

Job says to Eliphaz "teach me," which means that it is an argument between your lower self and your higher self or between you and your desire. You are Job trying to resolve the problem of suffering, sickness, and realize your heart's desire. You must reason with clarity of perception and the sword of spiritual awareness casting out all false theories, beliefs, and doctrines, and stand firm on the rock of One Spiritual Power—your own consciousness which is lord and master of your world. Cremate, burn up, consume incisively and decisively all negative thoughts, fears, doubts, anything and everything that challenges the realization of your desire. Realize omnipotence moves in your behalf and nothing can stay its power, therefore you wait joyously, patiently, and enthusiastically for the answered prayer.

7

Comments on Chapter 7, The Book of Job

(11) *Therefore I will not refrain my mouth; I will speak in the anguish of my spirit; I will complain in the bitterness of my soul.*

Here Job touches the depths. This is the time to look up unto God and the things that are God's, that is dedicate your thought, your desires, your plans to God and claim divine order, harmony, and love are flowing through you. As you do this, the Spirit will take you forward to victory, freedom, and accomplishment. "Why? Why?" was Job's cry as you find generally when misfortune comes upon people. The familiar echo is, "Why did God do this to me? I have been so good."

8

Comments on Chapter 8, The Book of Job

(1) Then answered Bildad the Shuhite, and said, (2) How long wilt thou speak these things? and how long shall the words of thy mouth be like a strong wind? (3) Doth God pervert judgment? or doth the Almighty pervert justice? (4) If thy children have sinned against him, and he have cast them away for their transgression;

Bildad means son of contention, the type of mind which believes you are being punished by God for your sins as set forth in many orthodox ecclesiastical theories. You are not punished for your sins but by your sins which is an automatic reaction of your subconscious to your habitual thinking. The word sin means to miss the mark or failure to get an answer to your prayer. Your sin is your failure to lead a full and happy life. When you fail to hit your mental target or the goal you set in life, you sinned, or missed your mark. Identify yourself mentally and emotionally with your ideal, exalt it in your mind, woo it, and claim it boldly, and the Almighty Power in you will respond and bring it to pass. All punishment and suffering are self-inflicted consciously or unconsciously.

There was a young boy, sixteen years old who constantly missed getting a job—there was always someone there before him. He missed his mark (job) about eight or nine times. He decided to pray about it, and on his next interview for a position he found there were fifteen other boys there. An idea emerged spontaneously from his subjective depths and he wrote it down on a piece of paper and gave it to the secretary who in turn gave it to the manager. He read the message which said, "I am the fifteenth boy in line, be sure you don't hire anyone until you see me." He got the job.

I talk to people who are ill and they say, "Oh, it is my karma. It is being accelerated because I am developing spiritually." Some are quite adamant and disputatious about these peculiar beliefs. This specious type of reasoning is designed to take you in and fool you. Many of these people have a martyr complex, and believe that God has singled them out for punishment for some inscrutable reason. This type of reasoning is indeed a poor comforter, nevertheless it is all too prevalent. Everything we experience is a reaction of our habitual thinking and beliefs, whether conscious or unconscious. We can experience nothing that is not a part of our own consciousness. Your state of consciousness is the way you think, feel, believe, and whatever you give mental consent. You are immersed in the collective unconscious mind into which all the people in the world are pouring forth their thoughts, beliefs, fears, hates, hopes, and irritations. All the intrigue, jealousy, invidious and iniquitous schemes hatched in the fetid brain of man are being sent forth into this mass mind also; you are a receiving and broadcasting station, and being in the race mind, you must keep prayed up, otherwise the fears, doubts, anxieties of the race mind will fill your mind and reach a point of precipitation coming forth as sickness, disappointment, and troubles of all kinds. It is just as essential to cleanse your mind as well as your body, otherwise your mind will get full of the mental debris of the world.

9

Comments on Chapter 9, The Book of Job

(16) If I had called, and he had answered me; yet would I not believe that he had hearkened unto my voice. (17) For he breaketh me with a tempest, and multiplieth my wounds without cause. (18) He will not suffer me to take my breath, but filleth me with bitterness.

Job bemoans his fate and finds no comfort or light in the orthodox mouthings of formal creeds which to him seem to be nothing but an opiate putting people asleep to the truth that God dwells in him and all His Wisdom, Power, and Love are available to man through His thought and feeling. If you postulate powers outside the one Power, you are no longer loyal to God, you no longer love God. To love is to be faithful, loyal, giving allegiance to the one Presence, then the Holy Spirit will move through you as health, harmony, peace, abundance, and security. You are here to sing the song of triumph. *When the morning stars sang together, and the sons of God shouted for joy!*

10

Comments on Chapter 10, The Book of Job

(8) *Thine hands have made me and fashioned me together round about; yet thou dost destroy me. (9) Remember, I beseech thee, that thou hast made me as the clay; and wilt thou bring me into dust again? (10) Hast thou not poured me out as milk, and curdled me like cheese?*

Here Job engages in a lot of self-pity and attributes all his misery to entire neglect on the part of God, and that after having created him, He does not take any notice of him. Dr. Phineas Parkhurst Quimby, the antecessor of mental and spiritual healing in this country, pointed out over a hundred years ago that your religious beliefs can cause diseases of all kinds. In analyzing the ailments of his patients, he discovered that their religious beliefs contained dangerous seeds of superstition, ignorance, and fear, all of which are highly detrimental to man's unfoldment.

Life is progression and all suffering and misery you have are due to Life's reaction to your failure to move onward and upward. Any mental retrogression or stagnation will bring about conflict and pain because you are here to grow, and if you are willful, self-satisfied, rebellious, and refuse to let life, love, truth, and beauty flow through you, pain is the result in order to remind you to remove the block and let the *healing forces* flow through you.

Dr. Quimby discovered that when false beliefs confine the God-Power, the phenomena known as disease occurs in the body forcing you to seek the cause of the trouble, and in so doing the process of growth is stimulated and carried on. The search like that of Job must forever continue until all men learn that the cause of all sickness and unhappiness originates in man's own mind. As you keep on seeking the answer a light will break. Faith, the know-how in Spirit will gain victory!

When you are depressed, despondent, and gloomy you must proceed to build a new mansion in the mind. Draw on the qualities which are resident within you. Begin to become amiable, sociable, kindly, and radiate good will to all; have faith in an everlasting Law which causes the sun to shine and brings the stars nightly to the sky. When you draw out the qualities of love, good will, and humor, you are building a new structure in your mind and you will inhabit this new building just the same as the man who is building a new home with bricks and stone will live in it.

11

Comments on Chapter 11, The Book of Job

(1) Then answered Zophar the Naamathite, and said, (5) But oh that God would speak, and open his lips against thee; (6) And that he would shew the secrets of wisdom, that they are double to that which is! Know therefore that God exacteth of thee less than thine iniquity deserveth. (7) Canst thou by searching find out God? canst thou find out the Almighty unto perfection?

Zophar means chirping, peeping, twittering; he is one of Job's three friends previously explained. We might elaborate a little further and say that these three friends, depicted as trying to comfort Job, merely represent phases of intellectual, traditional mental thought and false reasoning. This is why they fail to find any remedy for his afflictions. It is a case of the blind leading the blind, and they both fall into the ditch. They show Job that he is wrong, but cannot reveal the right way. Zophar is the type of mind that holds on to old, obsolete ideas and reasons from their standpoint he is seeking unto the dead.

The formal religionist will point out the evil appearances and condemn the sinner. Spiritual understanding alone gives the answer and shows you the way to peace, joy, and happiness. The enlightened or spiritually illumined mind holds up a spiritual standard for those he wishes to help instead of calling attention to and thereby magnifying apparent evil. Zophar reproves Job, saying in effect, "You are lucky it is not worse for God is exacting of you less than your sin deserves." What was Job's sin? He was using his mind wrongly, permitting beliefs and opinions of the world to muddy his consciousness and tip the scale in the wrong direction. Trouble comes to Job for he does not know how to control the conscious mind.

Zophar holds that God's will is the cause of everything that happens; no further cause can be sought for His actions, and it cannot be asked why He has done this and why He has not done that. In other words the Zophar state of consciousness says, "Don't try to understand God. It is too much for you. Just accept your ill fortune." This attitude is the typical three-dimensional objective consciousness, a matter-of-fact concrete approach which says you must not try to go into secret matters. The worldly materialistic type of mind is suspicious of mind phenomena and hence fights shy of all such ideas. It is true, of course, that the finite mind of man cannot completely comprehend the nature of God, for God is Infinite Being. *Canst thou by searching find out God? canst thou find out the Almighty unto perfection?*

(8) *It is as high as heaven; what canst thou do? deeper than hell; what canst thou know?*

While we cannot know all about God with our finite mind, we can learn much about the way it works in our own life. We can learn that Infinite Intelligence responds to the nature of our thoughts, that thoughts are things, that what we feel we attract, that what we contemplate we become, that any idea which we charge with feeling and enthusiasm will become objectified in our own life. There is much to learn about our subconscious mind and the way it works, and the study of our inner nature and laws of our being is endless.

12

Comments on Chapter 12, The Book of Job

(1) And Job answered and said, (2) No doubt but ye are the people, and wisdom shall die with you.

Job answers the bombastic and verbose Zophar rather sarcastically in what amounts to these terms, "You think that you know it all and wisdom shall die with you."

13

Comments on Chapter 13,
The Book of Job

(3) Surely I would speak to the Almighty, and I desire to reason with God. (4) But ye are forgers of lies, ye are all physicians of no value. (5) O that ye would altogether hold your peace! and it should be your wisdom.

In this chapter Job holds on desperately to his integrity (beingness). He would speak to the Almighty and desires to reason with God, but his friends (body, mind, and emotion) are forgers of lies. *O that ye* (fears, opinions, false beliefs) *would altogether hold your peace!* Be still, and it—this state of mental quietness and confidence in the presence of your good (God) should be your wisdom (right course of action). Job senses the very heart of spiritual demonstration, the secret of prayer which is to cleanse your mind of false beliefs, and what you need comes forth; for we must understand that in working with spiritual law we are bringing out concretely that which already is (as an idea, a seed which comes forth according to your mental acceptance). The sin of Job consisted essentially in magnifying obstacles, and so the thing he greatly feared came upon him.

(15) *Though he slay me, yet will I trust in him: but I will maintain mine own ways before him.*

Like a material scientist Job believes in the possibility of the execution of his idea; he is keeping up his search for the Great Cause—the One God who shall be his salvation.

14

Comments on Chapter 14, The Book of Job

(1) Man that is born of a woman is of few days, and full of trouble. (2) He cometh forth like a flower, and is cut down: he fleeth also as a shadow, and continueth not. (3) And dost thou open thine eyes upon such an one, and bringest me into judgment with thee? (4) Who can bring a clean thing out of an unclean? not one.

Job admits he does not understand the mystery of iniquity (how mind works). All those living in the race mind full of unknown fears, foreboding, false beliefs, etc., will be full of trouble until they awaken to the presence and power of God within them and redirect their thought life and emotions along God-like channels. All of us are born into limitation, i.e., we are born into the traditional beliefs of our parents and all that our environment represents. The child is subject to the mental atmosphere and emotional climate of the home. All of us are in a vast mental sea called the collective unconscious or race mind which impinges on our mind regularly until we awaken to the spiritual truth of our own sovereignty and take charge of our own mind; then we are born again into new mental and spiritual world.

You are born of woman (worldly beliefs, feelings, and prejudices) and full of trouble when you are unawakened to your spiritual capacities. When you take over the government of your mind you will immediately eradicate and expunge from your consciousness all false beliefs, fears, hates, and bickerings—disease and misery will vanish away.

To change your mind is to change your world and you do this by trusting the One Spiritual Power which you can contact through your thought rejecting completely all belief in powers outside your own consciousness. You will come to the conclusion that your consciousness is God relative to your world, and that everything you experience comes forth from your consciousness which is the sum total of your conscious and subconscious beliefs.

15

Comments on Chapter 15, The Book of Job

(6) Thine own mouth condemneth thee, and not I: yea, thine own lips testify against thee. (7) Art thou the first man that was born? or wast thou made before the hills?

"Cheer up," says Eliphaz, "Don't complain, others went through this before you were born." The discourse of Eliphaz in chapter fifteen is banal, boresome, and didactic. He holds that the fate of Job was in accordance with strict justice, that Job was guilty of sins for which he deserved his fate. Eliphaz therefore says to Job, "Is not thy wickedness great, and thine iniquities infinite?"

(14) What is man, that he should be clean? and he which is born of a woman, that he should be righteous?

(15) *Behold he putteth no trust in his saints; yea, the heavens are not clean in his sight.* (16) *How much more abominable and filthy is man, which drinketh iniquity like water?*

The blatant, iniquitous, and mordant mouthings of Eliphaz are repulsive to the Inner Self. No wonder Job, in chapter sixteen, verses one and two says, "I have heard many such things: miserable comforters are ye all." These comforters are miserable because they do not know how to explain to Job the meaning of *Except ye repent, ye shall likewise perish.* Except you change your mind, get a new concept of God and a new interpretation of life, and begin to think in a new way, change your thought and keep it changed, you too, will be subject to the law of averages, or the importations from the race mind which reach a climax in our mind bringing all kinds of trouble in their train. You must keep prayed up and establish counter convictions to all the race mind beliefs. The word repent means to think in a new way, to turn back to God, and to think God's thoughts after him.

16

Comments on Chapter 16, The Book of Job

(4) I also could speak as ye do: if your soul were in my soul's stead, I could heap up words against you, and shake mine head at you.

Job says he could speak idly to no real purpose. He is weary of the explanation that his woes are due to his wickedness.

17

Comments on Chapter 19, The Book of Job

(16) I called my servant, and he gave me no answer; I intreated him with my mouth. (17) My breath is strange to my wife, though I intreated for the children's sake of mine own body. (20) My bone cleaveth to my skin and to my flesh, and I am escaped with the skin of my teeth. (21) Have pity upon me, O ye my friends; for the hand of God hath touched me.

To his desperate appeal for help, Job perceives the invidious and specious type of reasoning and realizes it is nothing but pollyannish pratings about "God is Love," and all will be right eventually. Leverage is lacking. Job still does not know the science of mind, and how it works.

He calls his servant (mind), and gets no answer. His mental attitude is not yet conditioned to confidence in the One Spiritual Power within him. His breath is strange to his wife. Your wife is the ideal you wish to marry mentally and emotionally unite with. Like Job you might like to marry or unite with the idea of perfect health. You have to get into the feeling of health, and as you begin to rejoice in the fact that the Infinite Healing Presence is now restoring you to perfection, you will get the feeling of health, and the feeling of health produces health in the same manner as the feeling of wealth produces wealth.

Job's breath (his life force, enthusiasm, faith) has not yet been infused into his idea or desire; he has not yet surrendered mentally to the Omnipotence of God. Hence, even his familiar friends—*My familiar friends have forgotten me*—verse fourteen—(sense of security, health, peace) have forgotten him inasmuch as he is incapable of believing in these qualities of God in his heart.

(25) *For I know that my redeemer liveth, and that he shall stand at the latter day upon the earth.*

Job senses intuitively now that his Redeemer (the Presence of God) liveth and that his awareness of the Intelligence and Wisdom of God within him and his faith in Its response to his prayer shall stand at the latter day upon the earth. All of which means that he shall experience on the outside (his body and environment) what he feels and claims as true on the inside.

(26) *And though after my skin worms destroy this body, yet in my flesh shall I see God.*

Job senses something is stirring toward objective manifestation in much the same way as in embryology the child may have been conceived though to fleshly sense no signs are as yet in evidence. You should walk in confidence that your desire (seed) has taken root in your subjective mind which contains the Presence and Power of God, and that it will come forth in divine order.

(27) *Whom I shall see for myself, and mine eyes shall behold, and not another; though my reins be consumed within me.*

In all this Job begins to sense that men's religious discourse is not practical philosophy but he still must secure a point of leverage so that his ideals (his friends, his brethren, his kinsfolk, his familiar friend, his wife) will no longer deem him an alien in their sight. Job is still in that stage of consciousness wherein he feels like a city besieged like an alien among strangers. The basic truth that God is his consciousness has not yet been gained by Job.

(28) *But ye should say, Why persecute we him, seeing the root of the matter is found in me?*

Job is making good progress for he senses that the root of the matter (his troubles) is found in him (a negative state embodied in his subconscious mind which is not as yet cleansed by scientific prayer which is to mentally and emotionally unite with the qualities and attributes of God—his Redeemer).

18

Comments on Chapter 20, The Book of Job

(19) Because he hath oppressed and hath forsaken the poor; because he hath violently taken away an house which he builded not; (20) Surely he shall not feel quietness in his belly, he shall not save of that which he desired.

In verse nineteen *the poor* refer to the dreams, aspirations you have had but were left to starve for want of faith in the unseen potencies of the Spirit within you.

Verse twenty means your emotional life (belly) is disturbed because you failed to realize your desires and ambitions.

19

Comments on Chapter 22, The Book of Job

(1) Then Eliphaz the Temanite answered and said, (5) Is not thy wickedness great? and thine iniquities infinite? (6) For thou hast taken a pledge from thy brother for nought, and stripped the naked of their clothing. (9) Thou hast sent widows away empty, and the arms of the fatherless have been broken. (10) Therefore snares are round about thee, and sudden fear troubleth thee.

Eliphaz contends that God is impartial; hence it is man's fault that he experiences troubles. But Eliphaz does not understand the essential meaning and significance of spiritual sinning—looking for solutions of problems externally instead of seeking your good through a psychological identification with God through feeling the reality of what you are praying for. Your *feelings* and *convictions* become inevitably the *garments* you will wear. Hence, do not take a pledge for naught, i.e., do not condition your good on the outside, but claim your good on the inside or secret place, and whatever you claim and feel as true in your prayer process, Spirit will validate and objectify. Then you will not strip the naked (your desires) of their clothing (feelings of conviction of their reality in your own consciousness).

Widows are lost ideals which we have given up hope of realizing. These ideals should have been husbanded by faith and love into outward existence. You can demonstrate anything you can enclose with your faith (feeling). Your desire must be married to your faith. Know that desire is God coming to you in form of your needs (your bread). The crucial test in all this is the challenge to your spiritual understanding. God is your consciousness! Do you sense the reality of this metaphysical position? Hence, be about your Father's business (feel health, bliss, wealth, etc.), and the rest will follow in due course based on the law of mental acceptance which you have called into operation.

The word *man* in the Bible means mind, the measurer. This mind must cease being born of woman (race mind, irrational moods and fears) as explained previously. We shall experience plenty of trouble if we do not do our own planning, choosing, and directing. Our mind is born of God when Wisdom takes over and we base our spiritual standard on whatsoever things are true, lovely, just, and of good report. You must cease being one of the herd subject to the law of averages. Let the government of your mind be controlled by divine ideas; then you will be born of the true woman which is wisdom or intuition.

(21) *Acquaint now thyself with him, and be at peace: thereby good shall come unto thee.* (22) *Receive, I pray thee, the law from his mouth, and lay up his words in thine heart.* (23) *If thou return to the Almighty, thou shalt be built up, thou shalt put away iniquity far from thy tabernacles.* (24) *Then shalt thou lay up gold as dust, and the gold of Ophir as the stones of the brooks.*

You have to get acquainted with the fact that there is but one Creative Principle, and then realize that when you think the One Power is responding to you, as you contemplate the great truth that the Supreme Power is now functioning in your behalf, you are assured of success and triumph. When negative thoughts or opposing factors come to your mind, reject them completely by recalling that they are shadows of the mind, and a shadow has no real home.

They are illusions of power; the power is in your own thought and consciousness. Fear, doubt, and worry are merely suggestions of power and cannot do any harm to you except you give them power.

There is a simple way in which you can acquaint yourself with this Power. A man in our class decided to give up smoking, and at night prior to sleep he said, "I am free from this habit, completely free through the Power of the Almighty which takes away all craving." He repeated this phrase a few times to himself and then went off to sleep dwelling on the one word *freedom* which he repeated over and over again like a lullaby. He lost all desire for cigarettes. He became acquainted with the powers within him. His subconscious mind was reactive to thought, and when he definitely came to a decision in his conscious mind that he wanted to be completely free from the habit, then the Power of the Almighty was resurrected and flowed in response to his decision.

An actress who was out of work for six months, pictured herself singing before a microphone, felt the reality of it, gave her attention and devotion to this mental image exalting it in her mind until it began to fascinate and enthrall her. The idea began to captivate her mind, and she became emotionally attached to it, and went off to sleep feeling the contract in her hand. She repeated this technique regularly every night for about a week. Suddenly she had no further desire to pray about it for the simple reason she had succeeded in impregnating her subconscious mind. Her picture had jelled, she had built it up thought by thought, picture upon picture, mood upon mood until the mental image became a subjective embodiment.*

Thoreau said that any man could bring anything he wanted into his life by having a picture of it and by filling that picture with faith. Faith is simply an awareness that that which you are praying for already is; the mere fact you desire it proves that it exists. As you begin to acquaint yourself with this Power you will discover that when you call upon God, He will answer you; if you pray for right action, you will experience a reaction and deep response of well being within yourself. An All-Wise Being will take over and compel you to give a good account of yourself.

(23) *If thou return to the Almighty, thou shalt be built up.*

This means that the God-Presence in you is always responsive and reactive; if you want more energy, a healing, or what not, this Almighty Power which moves the world will restore, repay, and satisfy you according to the nature of your request. Einstein pointed out how he received answers from his deeper

* See chapter on IMAGINATION AND SUCCESS in *Believe in Yourself.*

mind. He said, "I listened for an answer, for every bit of evidence, every bit of light, and every little thread of guidance, and I began to realize that these threads of thought and inspiration began to weave themselves together, and as I continued to listen, the whole pattern was fabricated in my mind and I had the answer, I had the formula."

(28) *Thou shalt also decree a thing, and it shall be established unto thee: and the light shall shine upon thy ways.* (29) *When men are cast down, then thou shalt say, There is lifting up; and he shall save the humble person.*

If you are depressed, return to the Almighty and affirm that God is with you. Decree boldly that Almighty God is your silent partner, your invisible friend and that He is your divine companion, and that he careth for you. The reason you are cast down or depressed, disconsolate, or discouraged is because you wandered away psychologically from God, you went out into the periphery of life, and the shadows began to fall; the closer to God the fewer the shadows, and the more light in your mind. Instead of living in gloom, thou shalt decree, "I live with God."

They have occupational therapy in many hospitals where they put morbid, depressed mental cases to work in weaving baskets, making leather bags, chairs, etc. Many of these people experience wonderful healings because this constructive type of work takes them out of their morbidity and their gruesome attitude into function, expression, and creativity; they are doing something for others and at the same time releasing their hidden talents.

20

Comments on Chapter 23, The Book of Job

(8) Behold, I go forward, but he is not there; and backward, but I cannot perceive him: (9) On the left hand, where he doth work, but I cannot behold him: he hideth himself on the right hand, that I cannot see him:

Job is discerning higher truths in these verses; the *left hand* is the subjective or subconscious mind which responds to your prayer according to the impression made upon it. You do not see the working of your deeper mind, and you do not know how your prayer will be answered; that is the secret of the subconscious or subjective mind which is the creative medium or Law of God in you. The subconscious is not God, but it is a part of God or the law which responds to our imagery and mental acceptance.

In the prayer process you see the beginning and the end, but you do not see the manner or creative process of unfoldment. You place a seed in the ground, but actually you do not know how it grows, the acorn becomes the oak according to a subjective wisdom inherent in the seed. You cannot see the growth of the embryonic idea in your mind, but you know it has its own plan and power of expression, that its mathematics and mechanics come with it. All you do is nourish your seed (idea, desire) and water it with your contemplation, picturing the happy ending or glorious fulfillment.

The *right hand* mentioned in verse nine means the manifestation of your desire.

(10) *But he knoweth the way that I take: when he hath tried me, I shall come forth as gold.*

Job senses his essential spiritual integrity for he shall come forth as gold (spiritual reality).

21

Comments on Chapter 24, The Book of Job

(1) Why, seeing times are not hidden from the Almighty, do they that know him not see his days? (2) Some remove the landmarks; they violently take away flocks, and feed thereof.

Times are not hidden from the Almighty which represent the cycle of sequence from embryonic idea to manifest form. In other words, the sequence of action between cause and effect is known to your Deeper Mind. *Days* mean the positive effects or major objectives. So long as you are asleep to the Truth of Being, you cannot read the times in the sense that you must take what comes except you meditate, pray, and let God's Wisdom guide, direct, and watch over you in all your ways.

You will know what to expect if you plant wonderful seeds (thoughts) of peace, health, happiness, joy, good will, and humor in your mind regularly and systematically. The future is always the present grown up, the invisible thoughts we dwell on become visible in experience and events. When you meditate on whatsoever things are lovely and of good report, you are assured of a wonderful future. Cause is your mental action and effect is the automatic response of your subconscious mind called the Law.

In verse two, you remove your *landmarks* when you reject ideas which hold you in bondage. Your concept, your real estimate of yourself defines the state of mind or mansion in which you dwell. Change your concept of yourself, and you change your destiny.

22

Comments on Chapter 25, The Book of Job

(1) Then answered Bildad the Shuhite, and said, (2) Dominion and fear are with him, he maketh peace in his high places. (3) Is there any number of his armies? and upon whom doth not his light arise? (4) How then can man be justified with God? or how can he be clean that is born of a woman? (5) Behold even to the moon, and it shineth not; yea, the stars are not pure in his sight. (6) How much less man, that is a worm? and the son of man, which is a worm?

Man is like a worm in the sense that he crawls along the earth being a victim of circumstances and conditions and a prisoner of fear, lack, and limitation. Man is born to soar aloft above all problems, to use the wings of disciplined imagination and faith, and transcend the difficulty. You must never permit your mind to crawl before facts and events of life, rather you must rise triumphantly, and imagine the desired end, and move toward it with faith and confidence thereby bringing you new life and happiness.

The eagle is a bird that soars aloft above the storm and looks directly into the face of the sun; this is why the eagle is a symbol for America, to remind you that you are to look to God, or the sun of your life, by contemplating the divine solution through the wisdom of the Almighty. *I bare you on eagles' wings, and brought you unto myself.*

Psychologically Bildad is right, for he (Job) is beginning to sense that man can be double-minded living with dominion or fear, and man is but a worm when he does not yet understand his oneness with God. Bildad's quandary is significant. How can man (unillumined) be justified with God? or how can he be clean (in mind) that is born of a woman (receptive feeling to the fears, hates, jealousies, etc., of the world) wherein the subconscious mind becomes filled with the negative impressions from the world of opinions, ignorance, and falsehoods.

23

Comments on Chapter 26, The Book of Job

(1) But Job answered and said, (2) How hast thou helped him that is without power? how savest thou the arm that hath no strength? (14) Lo, these are parts of his ways: but how little a portion is heard of him? but the thunder of his power who can understand?

Job now longs to ascend above mere manlike (worm-like) state of mind and wishes to understand the mystery of how *the arm that has no strength* can be saved. In verse fourteen, Job senses that he knows but parts of God's ways, the *thunder* (actions) of His power, who can understand?

Job now begins to strike fire in his meditations on the stirrings of the Spirit within him. He now feels that to know *Alpha* will initiate the sequence to *Omega* (manifestation). *Alpha* means your desire or the voice of God; the manner of manifestation is not for man to inquire. We must learn how to feel the reality of the wish fulfilled in order to possess or experience it on the screen of space. Your desire must be married to your feeling, and then there follows a subconscious embodiment resulting in the answer to your prayer.

24

Comments on Chapter 28, The Book of Job

(1) Surely there is a vein for the silver, and a place for gold where they fine it. (2) Iron is taken out of the earth, and brass is molten out of the stone. (6) The stones of it are the place of sapphires; and it hath dust of gold. (7) There is a path which no fowl knoweth, and which the vulture's eye hath not seen.

In these verses the inspired writer is telling you of the sapphires and gold hidden in the depths of yourself. Your deeper mind contains the limit less treasures of the Infinite One. The jewels of eternity are locked within man such as Boundless Wisdom, Indescribable Beauty, Absolute Love, Absolute Harmony, Infinite Intelligence, Absolute Bliss. *Eye hath not seen nor ear heard, neither hath it entered into the heart of man the things which God hath prepared for those who love Him.* Never in eternity could you exhaust the glories and beauties that are within you. Contemplate the illimitable wonders that are within you, and you will be seized with a mystic awe—the wonder of it all.

In verse seven, *the path which no fowl knoweth* represents the nature of the boundless Wisdom within you. This subjective Wisdom has ways you know not of, and responds to you in a manner you expecteth not. The whole world could tell you that something you planned was impossible, but the boundless Wisdom within you knows the way and reveals the perfect plan. The vulture may see the dead body many miles away and is led to it by a subjective radar system, but there is a Wisdom within you that transcends the instinctual wisdom of all the birds and beasts of the field—that of the Infinite Knower. All that is necessary is to trust and believe, and the answer comes forth like the sun in the morning.

(12) *But where shall wisdom be found? and where is the place of understanding?* (13) *Man knoweth not the price thereof; neither is it found in the land of the living.* (15) *It cannot be gotten for gold, neither shall silver be weighed for the price thereof.* (19) *The topaz of Ethiopia shall not equal it, neither shall it be valued with pure gold.* (20) *Whence then cometh wisdom? and where is*

the place of understanding? (28) And unto man he said, Behold, the fear of the Lord, that is wisdom; and to depart from evil is understanding.

The greatest thing in all the world is wisdom. If a man possessed wisdom, he would not need wealth, health, or peace of mind; he would have the know-how of accomplishment. Wisdom is greater than a healing because if you had wisdom, you would not need a healing. You have wisdom when you are aware of the Presence and Power of God within you, and your capacity to contact and release limitless treasures into your experience and conditions of life. You possess wisdom when you know that thoughts are things, that what you feel you attract, that what you contemplate you become, that what you imagine and feel you create.

Wisdom transcends the intellect; the latter is used to carry out the dictates of the Divine. Wisdom is the Presence of God in you. It is the Healing Presence. Wisdom knows all and sees all. It knows all the processes and functions of your body and knows exactly how to heal. If you go into business you can call on the Infinite Wisdom to give you new creative ideas, to prosper and guide you, and if you simply trust and believe in Its responsiveness, you will receive a thousand fold.

The fear of the Lord that is wisdom. The word fear means to have a healthy reverence and respect for the power of God within, to give it your supreme allegiance and know no other. Know, therefore, that the Power that moves the world is back of you on no other condition than that you call cheerfully, optimistically, joyously on the God Wisdom within. You will receive lavishly and beyond your fondest dreams. You possess Wisdom, the Pearl of Great Price, when you place all your reliance upon the Spirit within knowing that because God knows the answer you, therefore, must also know the answer. This attitude of mind will bring forth spontaneously from your subliminal depths the joy of the answered prayer.

Surrender yourself to the God-Wisdom and affirm boldly, "God leads, guides, governs, and prospers me in all my undertakings. I predicate my success, happiness, and achievements on the fact that Wisdom reigns supreme."

You will be amazed to discover that you will be possessed with a mental acumen, an amazing sagacity enabling you to bring order, symmetry, beauty, and balance into all phases of your life. You will be automatically led and protected in all your investments, and you will intuitively perceive tremendous potentialities where others see nothing.

Wisdom means you have chosen God and His Infinite Goodness to control your life and be your manager, counsellor, guide, and friend. You possess

Wisdom when you allow God to be your Loving Father who cares for you and pours out His beneficent rays of love and light on you whether asleep or awake. When your thoughts are true and Godlike, you secrete love in your heart which is the chalice of His Love; when your emotions and feeling (nature) are controlled by God's ideas, you are at peace with the world; when you have Love for your mother or feeling (nature) your heart is full of understanding. You stand under the Law of Love—*to depart from evil is understanding.*

Stand on the platform of God is Love, and Love is the fulfilling of the Law. A man said to me recently that he had suffered obloquies and objurgations at the hands of his employer; he was very bitter and hostile saying that the duplicity and rapacity of his boss knew no bounds. This man was sick mentally and physically because of his odium for his employer. He began to acquire wisdom which has nothing to do with the accretion of facts and formula, but rather with the working of an Infinite Principle of Life within him. He recognized that he had the power to command his own mental reactions according to the Law of Harmony and Peace; he realized that the statements or criticisms of his boss continually heaped upon him could not possibly disturb him except through the medium of his thought. He took charge of his thoughts and kept them aligned with the Law of Love and the Golden Rule, and a healing followed.

He identified with his aim in life and refused to give any person, condition, or circumstance the power or prerogative to cause him to deflect from his aim. He made it a habit to identify with his aim which was peace, tranquility, serenity, joy, and harmony. This process is called the Wisdom of God operating in the mind of man. God's Love in you transmutes everything that touches your mind into love; this is why it is written that *all things work together for good to them that love God.*

25

Comments on Chapter 29, The Book of Job

(1) Moreover Job continued his parable, and said, (2) Oh that I were as in months past, as in the days when God preserved me; (3) When his candle shined upon my head, and when by his light I walked through darkness; (4) As I was in the days of my youth, when the secret of God was upon my tabernacle; (5) When the Almighty was yet with me, when my children were about me; (6) When I washed my steps with butter, and the rock poured me out rivers of oil.

The secret which Job speaks of is joy. You can capture your youth by stirring up the gift of God within you Every time you recognize the spirit within as Lord Omnipotent and reject the power of false beliefs of the world you are stirring up the gift of God within you. You can now feel the Miraculous, Healing, Self-Renewing, Ever-Living God moving through your mind and body. Feel and know that God is inspiring, rejuvenating, and strengthening you. As you continue to affirm these truths from the standpoint of the Infinite One, you will become recharged and revitalized spiritually, mentally, and physically. You can bubble over with enthusiasm and joy as in the days of your youth for the simple reason you can always recapture the joyous state mentally and emotionally.

The *candle which shines upon your head* is Divine Intelligence which reveals to you everything you need to know and enables you to affirm the presence of your good regardless of appearances. Where there is lack, you can see abundance, for the Light is in your mind, and you are here to let that Light shine through you in all your undertakings. Where there is sorrow, you can see joy; where there is chaos and disorder, you in your mind's eye can see, know, and intuitively perceive God's order which reigns supreme. If the suggestion of impotency and other inhibitory thoughts come to your mind, you look above and beyond to the divine solution knowing that the Miraculous Power is now working, leading you to the place where your vision is. The intellect may not discover the answer, but your awareness of the creative Intelligence in you is the Light which you hold aloft. This Light is always a lamp unto your feet and a guide in the darkness. His candle is God's Wisdom which anoints your intellect, lighting up all the dark places of your mind, revealing to you the perfect plan and showing you the way you should go. You walk by His Light because you know the dawn appears and all the shadows flee away.

(14) *I put on righteousness, and it clothed me: my judgment was as a robe and a diadem.*

In verse fourteen you are always judging; your *judgment* is your thought, your decision, your conclusion. You choose that which is noble, lovely, and Godlike; then your judgment is true. There is always an automatic reaction of the Law of our subconscious to the conscious decision. Your judgment must be as the robe or Truth. The *diadem* is to realize beauty, order, symmetry, and proportion where the problem or difficulty is.

If your father is ill and you see him sick and hope he gets better, you have judged wrongly. If you see the Presence of God where he is and know that the Healing Presence is now saturating and penetrating every atom of his being and that the peace of God flows through his mind and body, your judgment is as a robe and a diadem. Your judgment is true, and as you continue to feel this mental and spiritual atmosphere of health, peace, and perfection for your father, you are seeing him as he ought to be, radiant, happy, and free.

You put on righteousness when you think right, feel right, do right, act right, and have the right relationship with God. You put on the garment or robe of righteousness when you claim Divine Order and Divine Right Action are now taking place, for Order is heaven's first Law.

Galvanize yourself into the feeling of being one with your desire and seal yourself in that conviction; you are now clothed in righteousness, and your judgment is as a robe and a diadem. It is wonderful!

(15) *I was eyes to the blind, and feet was I to the lame.*

You are *blind* Biblically speaking when you say that you cannot solve your problem or that there is no way out of your dilemma. Your spiritual awareness enables you to know that your changed consciousness changes conditions and circumstances, and that no matter what the problem or difficulty may be, you can visualize and contemplate the solution and see the way you want it to be. As you continue to dwell in this mental atmosphere, the dawn appears and the shadows flee away. Divine Intelligence will shine through you guiding and revealing to you the perfect plan. You are lame if you are afraid to move forward to your goal. Many people hesitate, halt, and retreat when they meet with obstacles and set backs.

Feet means understanding, and you become *feet to the lame* when you stand firmly on the rock of Truth knowing that what you accept, and agree within your mind must come to pass. Remain on the rock and refuse to be swayed, moved, or frightened; you position is unassailable, and victory is assured, for according to your faith (mental acceptance) is it done unto you.

The Creative Intelligence within you is the Light that lighteth every man that cometh into the world. This Light in your mind determines what you see, and you are always seeing tremendous potentialities for yourself and others.

26

Comments on Chapter 31, The Book of Job

(1) I made a covenant with mine eyes; why then should I think upon a maid? (2) For what portion of God is there from above? and what inheritance of the Almighty from on high? (3) Is not destruction to the wicked? and a strange punishment to the workers of iniquity? (4) Doth not he see my ways, and count all my steps? (5) If I have walked with vanity, or if my foot hath hasted to deceit; (6) Let me be weighed in an even balance, that God may know mine integrity.

Job is still puzzled as to the causes behind all the evil happenstance and circumstances. This is truly a hard lesson for Job to learn. He does not yet know that his subconscious mind is no respecter of persons, and if he lies down in the bed of his mind and unites mentally and emotionally with evil thoughts and destructive concepts, he will spawn an evil progeny. Job must die to the old conception of the belief in the tree of good and evil (two powers or duality) and become acquainted with the One Power which through law manifests in the image and likeness of that which is planted therein by the unillumined conscious mind.

(9) *If mine heart have been deceived by a woman, or if I have laid wait at my neighbour's door.*

Job's mistakes were in the last analysis not due to outer impropriety but to inner ignorance of the source of his integrity—God. He did not as yet see the truth, as Job must die psychologically by arriving at a point or place in consciousness where the conscious mind ceases to be active in the squirrel cage of mere opinion and worry and become still in God and receptive to His Wisdom. Job must learn to let Infinite Intelligence lead, guide, and master his life.

(19) *If I have seen any perish for want of clothing, or any poor without covering;* (20) *If his loins have not blessed me, and if he were not warmed with the fleece of my sheep.*

Job may have *warmed the needy* in his geographical neighborhood with the fleece of his sheep, he did psychologically and spiritually speaking fail to *warm* emotionally in happy mood his ideals and desires.

These poor ideas were indeed left to freeze for want of the warmth of the fleece of his sheep (moods of joy and expectancy of the best). He proved but a poor shepherd of his sheep (feelings and moods).

Job says that he has always *clothed the naked and clothed the poor.* You will always hear that familiar cry from people everywhere such as, "I have always given to the poor, contributed to charities. I go to church regularly. I have been kind to people, etc." You must remember that they have forgotten to clothe their desires, ideals, and the aspirations of their hearts. They failed to give attention, love, and devotion to the spiritual values of life, or they neglected to worship the One True God. Many good people are good in the sense that they contribute to society and lead a good respectable life from a worldly standpoint, but their relationship to God may be very unfriendly, such as living in constant fear of reverses, or punishment by God for sins committed, or harboring secret fears, jealousies, and hates. You must worship, love, and make alive the qualities, attributes, and aspects of God. The fatherless and the widows are within because you have not fathered and mothered the cherished dreams of your heart and made a hospitable mental home for your inner urges and aspirations.

(24) *If I have made gold my hope, or have said to the fine gold, Thou art my confidence.*

Job should have made the *gold* of Wisdom his hope instead of the *gold* of intellect.

(27) *And my heart hath been secretly enticed, or my mouth hath kissed my hand.*

Job should not have *kissed his hand* in pride of self-conceit, but should have kissed or mentally united with his desire for perfect health. In this connection read Psalm 2:12. *Kiss the Son* (becoming one with your ideal) *lest he be angry, and ye perish from the way, when his wrath is kindled but a little. Blessed are all they that put their trust in him.*

(40) *Let thistles grow instead of wheat, and cockle instead of barley. The words of Job are ended.*

The words of Job, the bound man, are ended. The old man of opinion who at times sees but through a glass darkly must now give way to a new Job, speaking in chapter thirty-two, through Elihu which means *Thy God Who Is.*

27
Comments on Chapter 32, The Book of Job

(1) So these three men ceased to answer Job, because he was righteous in his own eyes. (2) Then was kindled the wrath of Elihu the son of Barachel the Buzite, of the kindred of Ram: against Job was his wrath kindled, because he justified himself rather than God. (3) Also against his three friends was his wrath kindled, because they had found no answer, and yet had condemned Job.

The words of Job are ended. Through the stage of consciousness denoted by the name or term *Elihu*, Job comes to himself, finds his integrity, wholeness or oneness with God, and kindles his wrath against the old Job who persisted usually in justifying and rationalizing his condition rather than seeking for the

Infinite Healing Presence within him. Psychologically expressed—when the conscious mind (Job arguing and self-pitying) falls asleep; Elihu, the sense of being one with God, awakens. The name Elihu signifies the recognition by man that his Higher Self, the I AM, is God, and that when you say, I AM you are veritably announcing the presence and power of God as your inner reality.

(7) *I said, Days should speak, and multitude of years should teach wisdom.* (8) *But there is a spirit in man: and the inspiration of the Almighty giveth them understanding.* (9) *Great men are not always wise: neither do the aged understand judgment.*

You do not necessarily learn from experience, hence mere agedness does not always betoken wisdom. So long as you neglect to give attention to God and His Wisdom, you will be praying amiss. The judgment spoken of in verse nine is your mental estimate, your conviction, your blueprint of yourself which you take into your own consciousness, and the impressions and awarenesses which comprise your state of consciousness are always reflected on the screen of space. When you do not know that your consciousness is the causation factor behind everything that takes place in your experience, you have no understanding whether you are ninety or nine chronologically speaking.

(18) *For I am full of matter, the spirit within me con-straineth me.* (19) *Behold, my belly is as wine which hath no vent; it is ready to burst like new bottles.*

The *wine* spoken of is the wisdom of God which illumines the intellect and causes you to praise and exalt God in the midst of you. This wine is your new interpretation of life whereby you become enthusiastic, exhilarated, and God intoxicated. You are bubbling over with a joyous enthusiasm, seized with a divine frenzy, a sort of mystic awe—the wonder of it all!

The Elihu state of consciousness will have no traffic but with God and His Omnipotence; hence Elihu is ready to burst like new bottles and give vent to love and freedom.

(21) *Let me not, I pray you, accept any man's person, neither let me give flattering titles unto man.*

Oftentimes in mediumistic and psychic trances you fail to contact the true Source of Wisdom and are often carried away by flattery and trickery. I AM or God gives no flattering titles unto man.

28

Comments on Chapter 33, The Book of Job

(1) Wherefore, Job, I pray thee, hear my speeches, and hearken to all my words. Behold, now I have opened my mouth, my tongue hath spoken in my mouth. (3) My words shall be of the uprightness of my heart: and my lips shall utter knowledge clearly. (4) The Spirit of God hath made me, and the breath of the Almighty hath given me life.

The voice of God (Elihu) now speaks from the subjective level and Job mentally and emotionally begins to feel the Presence of God—the Presence of harmony, health, peace, and joy in his heart. Job's life (conscious mind) utters knowledge clearly and is truly informed of the Spirit in man which giveth inspiration and understanding. Job does not have to listen to the tiresome and bombastic fulminations of his former comforters (false beliefs and opinions) because he has now awakened to the truth of Being. Like Job, your words are ended also when you reject and cast out of your mind all such beliefs that you are a victim of punishment, vengeance, or karma.

Silence the three comforters of creed, dogma, and tradition within yourself, let these old concepts no longer have any voice in you because they are forgers of lies. Let God alone speak in you, follow the orders of the Holy One, accept Holy Orders now, and yield yourself to God's Wisdom claiming, feeling, and knowing that you are a soldier of God carrying out His orders to bring beauty, order, love, harmony, and inspiration into your own life and that of everyone you meet. Be faithful to your assignment, and His Candle will shine upon your head, and by His Intelligence you will go through all darkness, and come out into the Light, Love, and Freedom of the Spirit into the glorious liberty of the son of God.

(14) *For God speaketh once, yea twice, yet man perceiveth it not.* (15) *In a dream, in a vision of the night, when deep sleep falleth upon men, in slumberings upon the bed;* (16) *Then he openeth the ears of men, and sealeth their instruction,* (17) *That he may withdraw man from his purpose, and hide pride from man.* (18) *He keepeth*

back his soul from the pit, and his life from perishing by the sword.

Verse fourteen is intended to remind you that God is always speaking, forever broadcasting His Truths to all men everywhere. The River of Infinite Mind full of Boundless Wisdom and Infinite Intelligence is flowing through you and all people everywhere at this moment and right where you are. You might be too busy to listen, but if you will still the wheels of your mind, you will hear what God has to say. Cease maundering and grumbling and asseverate—God knows the answer. and you are listening for it, and in the silence He speaks. How can you hear if you refuse to listen?

In verses fifteen and sixteen Job reminds you that you may get answers to your problems in a dream and in a vision of the night. The writer of this book has received many answers to prayer in the dream state. Every night you go to sleep you take your last waking concept with you into the deep where it is etched on the subconscious mind; in other words, the mood in which you go to sleep determines the experiences you shall have tomorrow and the next day and the next except you change your consciousness through prayer and meditation. Whatever you impress on your subconscious will be expressed as experience and events. Go to sleep feeling that your prayer is answered. Sleep brings counsel.

Dr. Bigelow of England did considerable research work on the mysteries of sleep, and he pointed out that in the sleep state nothing actually sleeps. Your heart, lungs, and all your vital organs keep on functioning as well as your optic, auditory, olfactory, and gustatory nerves.

The fourth Psalm says, *I will both lay me down in peace, and sleep: for thou, Lord, only makest me dwell in safety.*

Dr. Bigelow, in his research work, *Mystery of Sleep*, cites the case of Professor Agassiz, who received a remarkable answer to one of his perplexing problems in the sleep state.

"He had been for two weeks striving to decipher the somewhat obscure impression of a fossil fish on the stone slab in which it was preserved. Weary and perplexed, he put his work aside at last, and tried to dismiss it from his mind. Shortly after, he waked one night persuaded that while asleep he had seen his fish with all the missing features perfectly restored. But when he tried to hold and make fast the image it escaped him. Nevertheless, he went early to the Jardin des Plantes thinking that on looking anew at the impression he should see something which would put him on the track of his vision. In vain—the blurred record was as blank as ever. The next night he saw the fish again, but with no more satisfactory result. When he awoke it disappeared from his memory as before. Hoping that the same experience might be repeated, on the third night he placed a pencil and paper beside his bed before going to sleep.

"Accordingly, towards morning the fish reappeared in his dream, confusedly at first, but at last with such distinctness that he had no longer any doubt as to its zoological characters. Still half dreaming, in perfect darkness, he traced these characters on the sheet of paper at the bedside. In the morning he was surprised to see in his nocturnal sketch features which he thought it impossible the fossil itself should reveal. He hastened to the Jardin des Plantes, and, with his drawing as a guide, succeeded in chiselling away the surface of the stone under which portions of the fish proved to be hidden. When wholly exposed it corresponded with his dream and his drawing, and he succeeded in classifying it with ease."

I will illustrate how the wisdom of your subjective self can instruct you and give you guidance relative to your request for guidance as you go to sleep. Many years ago I was assigned to a very lucrative position in the Orient, and one night prior to sleep I prayed as follows: "Father, Thou knowest all things, reveal to me the right decision. Thank You for Thy guidance."

I repeated this simple prayer over and over again as a lullaby prior to sleep, and in a dream came the vivid realization of things to come two or three years hence. An old friend appeared in the dream and said, "Read these headlines—do not go!" The headlines related to war. Occasionally, the writer dreams literally. Moreover, the subjective mind of man always projects a person whom you will immediately obey because you trust and love that person. To some a warning may come in the form of a mother who appears in a dream. She tells them not to go here or there, and the reason for the warning. Your subjective is all-wise. It knows all things. It will speak to you only in a voice that your conscious mind will immediately accept as true. It would therefore not be someone whom you distrusted or disliked. Oftentimes the voice of a mother or loved one may cause you to stop on the street, and you find, if you had gone another foot, a falling object from a window might have struck you on the head. Now, this is not the voice of your mother, or teacher, or loved one, it is simply the voice of your own subjective and it speaks in a tone or sound that you instantly obey. As proof of this I questioned my friend, and he assured me that he knew absolutely nothing about the warning he had given me subjectively.

No, it is man's own subjective that is ever portraying the drama of its contents in the form of a dream or a vision of the night. If man suggests to himself that he will remember and understand the symbolism portrayed therein, he will know the outcome of many things, and he will also learn to change the dreams; for by changing his consciousness he changes the dream, and as he dreams, so shall he become.

Joseph was warned in a dream. God spoke to Solomon in a dream and offered him his choice of gifts. Solomon chose wisdom, and God added long life and riches. With all our getting, let us get understanding of this principle, and our pillars of strength will be the two great pillars, Boaz and Jachin—Wisdom and Understanding.

Possessing the wisdom which the Bible teaches and the understanding to apply the psychological principles therein, man's inner righteousness will show itself in the outer, and he will need no manmade rules of conduct to guide him, for he will be led by the wise Power within him. If the thing that you now want will bless yourself and others, then truly it is the Divine Will. *I am come that you might have life, and have it more abundantly.* Heretofore, you have asked for nothing, now ask that your joy might be full.

In prayer realize the great oneness, and feel the end of the answered prayer. The Being within you sees the beginning and also sees the end. It shows you the end in a feeling, in a dream, in a vision, or by a voice. Listen to It. It will talk to you. Obey It because It is

Wisdom speaking to you. *In a dream, in a vision of the night, when deep sleep falleth upon men in slumberings upon the bed; He openeth the ears of men and sealeth their instructions. He giveth to his beloved in sleep.*

The writer, in consequence of his dream, immediately cancelled the trip, cashed the tickets, and sought no reason. He was under subjective compulsion to do so. A subsequent event—the tragedy of Pearl Harbor proved the truth of the Inner Voice. *Trust in the Lord and do good. Thus shall ye walk in the land, verily ye shall be fed. Let Him be a lamp unto your feet.*

You are saved from the pit of sorrow, frustration, neuroses, mental aberrations of all kinds if you withdraw regularly and systematically from the vexations and strife of the day and commune regularly with God, seeking His strength, light, love, and peace. You save yourself from the tensions and anxieties of the world by calling on the Divine Intelligence to lead, guide, govern, and direct you in all your ways. You spend one third of your life asleep, and the purpose of it is that you might receive instruction and guidance from God, and that you might participate in the wisdom and glory of God.

Sleep is a divine ordinance and you cannot avoid it. Many answers are given you in sleep. Sleep is not just to rest the body, but is intended to withdraw your conscious mind from the worries, strife, and contention of the day, and seek solace, comfort, healing, and illumination in your union with God as you enter into the Holy of Holies each night. Every night of your life, as you go to sleep, you are going before the King of Kings and the Lord of Lords—God—the Living Spirit Almighty within you.

Be dressed for God mentally and emotionally. Go to sleep with the song of God in your heart, with love and good will for every living being in the world. Go into His presence clothed in the robes of love, peace, praise, and thanksgiving. You must be without spot or blemish when you visit God who is Absolute Love—the Immaculate Unblemished Presence. You must be all fair and no spot on thee. Wrap yourself in the mantle of Love, and go off to sleep with the praise of God forever on your lips.

You must remember there are many degrees of sleep, and every time you pray you are actually asleep to the world and alive to God. When you abstract your five senses from your problem or difficulty and focus all your attention on the solution or answer knowing that the subjective wisdom of God is bringing about a solution in ways you know not of; you are practicing the art of sleep as mentioned in the Bible. You are asleep to the falsehood and hypnotic influence of the world when you accept as true what your reason and senses deny. When you hear of a person getting a nervous breakdown, you are reading of one who wandered away from God, and has cohabited mentally and emotionally with the false gods of fear, worry, ill will, resentment, remorse, and confusion.

Withdraw regularly and systematically to your Divine Center and think, feel, and act from the standpoint of God and not from the standpoint of the superimposed structure of fear, ignorance, and superstition. All nature sleeps—flowers, trees, dogs, cats, insects, etc. Sleep is nature's soft nurse; it knits up the raveled sleeve of care. Healing takes place much quicker when you are asleep. The conscious mind is no longer arguing, worrying, fretting, fussing, and fuming; it is subjugated, abrogated, and suspended, and the Healing Presence works without any hindrance or negative patterns from the conscious mind. Remember that the future is already in your mind except you change it through prayer; there is nothing strange in the dream I had wherein I saw the headlines of the New York newspapers long before the second world war occurred. The war had already taken place in mind, and all the plans of attack were recorded on that great recording instrument, the subconscious mind or collective unconscious of the race. Tomorrow's events are in the higher dimension of your mind, so is next week and next year, and may be seen by a psychic or intuitive person.

None of these things seen can happen if you decide to pray; nothing is predetermined, foreordained. Your consciousness determines your destiny and your consciousness is the sum total of what you believe consciously and subconsciously. You can, therefore, through scientific prayer, mold, fashion, shape, and direct your own future, because you have decided to let God's Wisdom be your master, and His Wisdom leads you to ways of pleasantness and paths of peace. The mood in which you go to sleep tonight determines your tomorrow. Read a psalm prior to sleep. Dwell on these verses, *Bless the Lord, O my Soul and all that is within me. Bless His Holy Name.* You meet in life the affinities of the mood in which you went to sleep.

Dr. Emmet Fox, author of *Sermon on the Mount* and other popular books, told me that many of the greatest answers to his problems came to him in proverbs while he was sound asleep. He said the reason he probably received answers in his sleep was that he was at times too preoccupied with other things, and too busy objectively.

Tonight, as you go to sleep, feel that your prayer is answered and give thanks for the joy of the answered prayer for God knows only the answer. God giveth His beloved in sleep!

(23) *If there be a messenger with him, an interpreter, one among a thousand, to shew unto man his upright-*

ness: (24) *Then he is gracious unto him, and saith, Deliver him from going down to the pit: I have found a ransom.*

The messenger who acts as your ransom is your own awareness of the Indwelling God. The God Presence is submerged in your subconscious depths, and when you consciously contact the Infinite Intelligence and Boundless Love, you will heal the sick condition, overcome your sleeping infirmities, and banish fear and lack from your life. You will cease to sin or miss the target for which you aim, for you have discovered that the God Self in you cannot be sick, frustrated, or unhappy. You are already saved, and all you have to do is to participate through meditation in the Heavenly Presence, and you will discover the fields are already ripe to harvest.

Your awareness, belief, and confidence in your own I Amness will ransom you from fear, doubt, worry, sickness, or any kind of trouble. The price for freedom, happiness, and peace of mind is acceptance or belief. You must give up something to receive. To give is to receive. You must give up false beliefs in personal saviors and receive your Higher Self as your redeemer and liberator.

29

Comments on Chapter 34, The Book of Job

(29) When he giveth quietness, who then can make trouble? and when he hideth his face, who then can behold him? whether it be done against a nation, or against a man only.

No one can make trouble for you or disturb you without your mental consent. All the water in the ocean cannot sink a ship except the water gets inside, likewise no person, condition, or event can disturb you except you participate mentally and choose to get angry or hateful. You can choose to identify yourself with the God of Peace and let His River of Peace flow through you, identifying with your aim which is God and His Infinite Goodness, and refuse to identify with gloom, worry, self-pity, and self-criticism.

30

Comments on Chapter 36, The Book of Job

(3) I will fetch my knowledge from afar, and will ascribe righteousness to my Maker.

You are aware of the extraordinary powers of the Other Self in you. In Duke University and many other research laboratories throughout the world, they are demonstrating daily the powers of extra sensory perception, the capacity of your subjective mind to transcend time and space and reveal to you what is happening at a distance, and give you the answer to any problem, and fetch wisdom from afar, revealing to you anything you need to know at every moment of time and point of space.

(27) For he maketh small the drops of water: they pour down rain according to the vapour thereof: (28)

Which the clouds do drop and distil upon man abun-
dantly. (29) Also can any understand the spreadings of
the clouds, or the noise of his tabernacle? (30) Behold, he
spreadeth his light upon it, and covereth the bottom of
the sea. (31) For by them judgeth he the people; he giveth
meat in abundance. (32) With clouds he covereth the
light; and commandeth it not to shine by the cloud that
come betwixt. (33) The noise thereof sheweth concerning
it, the cattle also concerning the vapour.

Many people look upon these verses as very difficult
to interpret, yet they are extraordinarily simple when
you meditate on their meaning. The best way to read
any part of the Bible is to say to yourself, "What did I
mean when, as the writer of Job, I wrote these verses
thousands of years ago?" As you do this you are tuning
in on the receptive nature of the One Mind which wrote
all books, and its nature being responsiveness, you will
be governed accordingly. The key to the interpretation
of these passages is the mood which is psychological
vapor out of which rain, or the manifestation of your
ideal is precipitated as indicated in verse twenty-seven.

Verse twenty-eight. According to the cloud types
generated by your moods does *the rain drop and distil*
upon man abundantly, that is to say, all concrete man-
ifestations are determined by the quality of the vapor
clouds (mental emotional atmosphere) which arise in
man's consciousness (heavens).

Verse twenty-nine. *The noise of his tabernacle* reminds you that you are the tabernacle of the Living God, and the noise you experience is the sound of the answered prayer, or your deep conviction which like thunder presages what is coming, such as the precipitation of solids, or the external manifestation of your subconscious impregnation.

The great task for the student of truth is to translate physical things into their spiritual and psychological meanings. Fundamentally man is a microcosm in the area of which may be found even meteorological correspondences in the heavens (mind, consciousness, emotions). The spreading of the clouds is an allusion to mystic experiences when drawing nigh to the Holy One.

Verses thirty and thirty-one. Infinite Intelligence and Boundless Wisdom *covereth the bottom* (reside in your subconscious mind). The people referred to in verse thirty-one are symbolic of enthroned moods, attitudes, decisions, ideals. Your judgment is your mental decision or conclusion arrived at in your conscious reasoning mind. You hear the thunder, and then you see the rain. Hear the good news within yourself until you get the reaction which satisfies; this cloud or feeling covers or hides the manner of unfoldment or expression. You do not know how, when, where, or through what source your prayer will be answered. That is the secret of your Deeper Mind. It has ways you know not of, but you know it is going to rain for you because your consciousness is saturated and you are filled full of the feeling of being what you long to be.

Verse thirty-two reminds you that you are in the *clouds* when you are meditating, and whatever you qualify your consciousness with—that which is wonderful, noble, and Godlike, your Higher Self will pour out or rain blessings from heaven upon you. The two thunder gods are within you, James (righteous judgment) and John (love). When you come to a definite conclusion or decision in your conscious mind that your desire is good and of God, and that He will back you up, you are Job loving your ideal, and all the power of the Godhead flows to that focal point of attention, and you experience the joy of the answered prayer.

Verse thirty-three. *The noise thereof* (inner convictions) *sheweth* (manifests) concerning it (the concrete manifestation) precipitated after the thundering of the emotions in the heavens (consciousness); the *cattle* also (group of moods) are conditioned by the vapor (emotional moods) which precede the precipitation into form of the saturated clouds (movements of consciousness).

31

Comments on Chapter 37, The Book of Job

(1) At this also my heart trembleth, and is moved out of his place. (2) Hear attentively the noise of his voice, and the sound that goeth out of his mouth. (5) God thundereth marvellously with his voice; great things doeth he, which we cannot comprehend.

As a result of Elihu's deep wisdom, a complete change in consciousness is effected; the *heart* (subjective mind) is moved out of its place as the conscious mind lets go and allows the subjective wisdom to go into action. The voice of God is the feeling of peace that wells up with in you.

(7) He sealeth up the hand of every man; that all men may know his work. (8) Then the beasts go into dens, and remain in their places.

This means, as you go to sleep, assuming that God's Wisdom will solve your problem, then the *beasts will go into dens* meaning that all your troubles and worries will recede and be resolved peacefully through the wisdom and power of your subconscious mind. Before the *beasts* (worries and troubles) are liquidated you must learn to let go and let God act. You must not hang on to your negative experiences as the moth clings to the flame which consumes it if it be not redirected (by Law).

(9) *Out of the south cometh the whirlwind: and cold out of the north.*

The *south* means your emotional nature from which cometh the *whirlwind* (negative experiences), and cold out of the *north* (Higher Wisdom) which will resolve the difficulties. Your last waking concept is sealed in your subconscious mind, and the Higher Wisdom which resides in your subliminal depths will present you with an answer oftentimes in the morning provided you go to sleep knowing that God has the answer. If, in the morning you awaken with confidence, it is a good sign that the Law is at work on your needs.

(22) *Fair weather cometh out of the north: with God is terrible majesty.*

Fair weather means harmony comes out of the north (wisdom). When your conscious mind ceases to fret and worry, and you turn over your request to the God Wisdom within, the stars of Truth resident in your subconscious mind will shine, and in the morning you are presented with an answer. You will be convinced inwardly and indifferent to outward appearances. You know in your heart that prayer is accepting as true what your reason and senses deny.

32

Comments on Chapter 38, The Book of Job

(1) Then the Lord answered Job out of the whirlwind, and said, (2) Who is this that darkeneth counsel by words without knowledge? (3) Gird up now thy loins like a man; for I will demand of thee, and answer thou me. (4) Where wast thou when I laid the foundations of the earth? declare, if thou hast understanding. (5) Who hath laid the measures thereof, if thou knowest? or who hath stretched the line upon it? (6) Whereupon are the foundations thereof fastened? or who laid the corner stone thereof; (7) When the morning stars sang together, and all the sons of God shouted for joy?

This is not a question asked of God by Job, but it is really a question asked by man of his Higher Self.

You have forgotten who you are, and you are trying to remember. You have forgotten your divine origin and accepted the opinion of man as truth; consequently, you sin or err because you do not know that your own I AMness is the God that you seek. You dwell, therefore, in the land of many gods, and the belief in many powers. You were in the absolute state before you were born, and when you were born it was God appearing as a child.

All of us were born into the race mind, and to all that our environment represents. Original sin has nothing to do with the physical, sexual act; it is man believing in the wisdom of the world, opinions of man, and using his intellect destructively. The man who loves truth and practices the Presence of God is like a magnetized piece of steel. The man who is asleep to God is like a demagnetized piece of steel—the magnetic current is there, but it is asleep within him. When you contemplate the Presence of God, the electronic and atomic structure of your body reforms and vibrates accordingly. The real you within created the world and all things therein contained, and has a perfect memory of it. When you awaken to your divinity, you will realize that the whole world is within you.

Planets are thoughts, suns and moons are thoughts, and your own consciousness is the realization which sustains them all. Temporarily in space are moving the dreams of the dreamer, and the sun, moon, and stars are thoughts of the thinker. You come to the startling awareness that He is meditating and we are His meditations.

(32) *Canst thou bring forth Mazzaroth in his season? or canst thou guide Arcturus with his sons?* (33) *Knowest thou the ordinances of heaven? canst thou set the dominion thereof in the earth?*

Your Concordance gives you the key to these verses. *Mazzaroth* means the twelve powers or twelve faculties of mind within you. If you call forth these disciples or faculties and fully discipline them by prayer, meditation, and contemplation you will answer all the questions propounded in that wonderful thirty-eighth chapter of Job. You may call forth *Mazzaroth* by disciplining your twelve faculties as follows:

Reuben or *Andrew* means behold the Sun or God! *Andrew* means spiritual perception and is the first faculty of man. Spiritual seeing means understanding, illumination, and comprehension. This is not three dimensional seeing, but it is seeing the Truth about the outer fact. The spiritual person sees the law of cause and effect operating everywhere, and he knows there is a subjective pattern behind all manifestation in his body and affairs. He knows the realization of his desire is the Truth that sets him free.

We look at the atmosphere and we say that there is nothing there; yet it is teeming with life. We look into the heavens and we see stars, but when we look through the telescope, we see countless stars not discerned by the naked eye. Which is right, the telescope or the eye? Many think the sun rises in the East and sets in the West, but spiritual seeing or understanding knows that this is untrue.

If someone is sick in your family, how do you see them? If you see them unwell, you are not disciplining Andrew. Your spiritual perception or knowing must be a perfect vision of their health or happiness.

Do you resist, resent, or fight conditions in your home or office? If you do, you are not calling Andrew to discipleship. If you detach yourself from the problem and focus on your good, you are on the way towards mastering this power.

Peter is the second disciple or faculty of mind. *Peter* symbolizes the rock of Truth—an immutable conviction of good. Peter is the faculty of mind that reveals to man: *Thou art that Christ, the Son of the Living God.* JOHN 6:69. It reveals man's own I Amness is God, the Savior. Peter is faithful to the end. He is faithful every step of the way, knowing that Omnipotence is moving in his behalf, . . . *and that none can stay his hand, and say unto him, what doest thou?* DAN. 4:35.

Do you say to the ideal or desire murmuring in your heart, that, "I am too old. I do not have enough money. I do not know the right people"? Do you say, for example, that due to conditions, inflation, the present administration, events, or circumstances, it is impossible to realize your objective? If this is so, you are not disciplining Peter, but you are actually robbing yourself of the joy of experiencing your ideal. The faculty of faith (Peter) knows no obstacles and recognizes no master or Lord except his own I Amness. Do you pray for a little while, then give up and say, "I tried it, but it does not work"? If you do, you must begin now to call Peter to discipleship, and you will realize the cherished desire of your heart.

James is the righteous judge. *My judgment was a robe and a diadem.* JOB 29:14. This means that when we begin to discipline the faculty called James, we decree wholeness, completeness, and perfection. Our judgment (conviction) is the robe (Truth) and the diadem (beauty and perfection). We ask ourselves, "How is it in God and heaven?" Our inner realization is the Presence of God where the other is; thus our verdict or decree is Harmony, Health, and Peace.

Do you now condemn, criticize, or dwell on the shortcomings of others? If this is true, you are not calling James to discipleship, but you are actually building these negative qualities within yourself. We become that which we condemn. Look around and you will see ample evidence of this.

Are you incapable of hearing unpleasant things about another? Do you hear and realize only the good for the other? The student of Truth disciplining James never gossips, reproaches, or finds fault with people. If he hears gossip and it is true, the student rejects it mentally and never breathes a word of it. *Let none of you imagine evil against his neighbour.* ZECH. 8:17. Let us all call this faculty to discipleship.

John is the embodiment of love. Love is the spirit of God in action; love is also an emotional attachment. It is an at-one-ment with your ideal. *We know that all things work together for good to them that love God.* ROM. 8:28. Are you loving God now? God and good are identical and synonymous in all sacred scriptures. When we fall in love with these qualities and attributes, such as honesty, integrity, success, peace, forbearance, and justice, and when we love Truth for Truth's sake, we are loving God or Good.

Are you afraid of the future? Are you worried about your family, friends, or business? In short, are you unhappy? If you are, you can rest assured that you are not loving God or Good. You are loving limitations. Are you afraid of failure? If you have this fear, you will succeed in being a failure.

Do you hold a grudge towards any living being? If this is true, you are not controlling John. You must forgive the other, otherwise there is no love in your heart. Love the other by rejoicing that the person you say wronged you is living joyously and happily. Claim that the law of God is working for him, through him, all around him, and that peace fills his mind, body, and affairs. Can you now rejoice in hearing good news about your recent enemy? If you cannot, you are not in charge of this faculty. If you have failed to embody your ideal, you are not disciplining John.

Phillip means, spiritually, a lover of horses. A trainer of horses is firm but kind; he does not beat the horses, yet he lets the horses know he is master. The trainer is persistent; he has that quality which so many of us lack, i.e., stick-to-it-ive-ness. Phillip, therefore, is the faculty of mind within you that enables you to use the power you have through love; thus you conquer any situation.

At a rodeo you see a horse which is unbridled and untamed; no one can stay on him longer than a few seconds; this is the way with many people. You contemplate a new idea; you become enthused about it; a delightful mood is engendered. However, some one may sway you, or you may hear some unpleasant news which throws you off the horse (mood).

For example, a girl was contemplating a beautiful trip to Florida during war time. She had planned to visit some relatives near Miami. In the meantime she heard some girls remark how awful conditions were, the food was very bad, there was no possibility of swimming, and the prices were outrageous, etc. This resulted in the cancellation of the trip. Later she discovered she had made a great mistake. Since she had contemplated a delightful trip, and had lived in that joyous expectancy—*as within, so without*—a wonderful trip was in store for her. She permitted the negative suggestions of others to throw her off the lovely horse (mood) that she was riding.

Let us ride the mood, which means let us sustain it, and we will reach Jerusalem (the city of peace) within ourselves. In other words, it is the sustained mood that creates. Be faithful every step of the way to the end. You are master! You have been given dominion. Can you now be swayed or made to change your mind? Can negative suggestions, ridicule, and criticisms of others throw you off your horse? If this is true, you are not disciplining Phillip.

Does the death of one of your dear ones cause you to feel despondent and gloomy, or do you rejoice in their new birthday? If you feel dejected and gloomy, you are not calling Phillip to discipleship.

Bartholomew means, according to the Concordance, son of the furrowed, or son of the plowed, i.e., prepared for seed; spiritually, it represents imagination. This faculty has the power to cast every idea that man can conceive onto the screen of space in substance and form. The disciplined imagination (furrowed land or son of the furrowed) is capable of picturing only lovely states and delightful moods. Imagination and faith are the two pillars that lead to the Holy of Holies.

You call *Bartholomew* to discipleship when you imagine the reality of the fulfilled desire, and feel the joy of the answered prayer. If you are told of some evil prediction, it frightens you and you begin to imagine and conjure evil; you have not called forth this power. Do you imagine evil for another? Do you imagine that your son will fail in his examinations, or that something bad will happen to members of your family? If you have these negative patterns, you are failing to call this great faculty to discipleship. Let us imagine only the lovely, the beautiful, and the good qualities. Let our ideals be uplifted and let our judgment be as *the robe and the diadem.*

Thomas means jointed or conjoined. In the undisciplined state, it represents the double minded man, the doubter. It represents the understanding faculty of man. *Get wisdom and with all thy getting, get under-*

standing. PROV. 4:7. Wisdom is the knowledge of God; understanding is the application of this knowledge to solve our daily problems and grow spiritually.

Your reason and intellectual perception of the Truth becomes anointed by the Holy Spirit, and you go from glory to glory. The man who disciplines this faculty, Thomas, knows that his own consciousness or awareness is the God of his world and the seat of causation. He rejects, therefore, all rumors, lies, and suggestions that are unlike God or the Truth. He will contradict, reject, and refuse to accept any rumors of suggestions that oppose that which he knows to be true. How is it in God and heaven?

Does the polio scare that is given wide publicity disturb or frighten you? Do you send your children to some remote spot to escape the so-called peril? If this is true about you, you are full of fear, your faith is not in God or Good, and you do not believe in the Omnipresence of God. If you are calling Thomas to discipleship, you know that God is where you stand. He walks and talks in you. You are the very garment which God wears, as he moves through the illusion of time and space. Let us discipline Thomas; then we will touch Reality and know that God is.

Matthew means the gift of Jehovah, given wholly unto Jehovah; in short, Matthew means your desire. It is the cosmic urge within you seeking to be expressed.

Every problem has within it the solution in the form of a desire. If a man is sick, he automatically desires health. The desire (Matthew) is already knocking at this man's door; the acceptance of the desire is the answered prayer.

Do you say, "I am too old." "I lack the intelligence." "It is too late now." "I have no chance." Do you accept the verdict of the doctor or the race belief, or do you go within and say, like many of old, *My soul doth magnify the Lord?* LUKE 1:46. Yes, do you go within the silence, and magnify the possibility of realizing it? If you do, you are calling Matthew into discipleship. When you reject your desire, the gift of God which would bless you and the world, you are not calling Matthew to discipleship.

James the Less Matt. 10:3, *Mark* 15:40, signifies the faculty of order, or a tidy mind. Order is heaven's first law. When we are at peace in our minds, we find peace in our home, business, and in the rest of our affairs. This faculty of the mind is also called discernment or discrimination.

Quimby, the father of New Thought in America, had this quality of discernment highly developed. He was able to diagnose and interpret all of the causes behind the ailments or maladies of his patients. He told them where their pains and aches were, and the mental patterns behind them. We go to a doctor and tell him all of our symptoms, their location, etc., but Quimby did the reverse; he told the patient. They marvelled at this great capacity; he simply tuned in on their subconscious minds and subjectively saw their mental patterns. His explanation was the cure. Quimby was clairvoyant. When this clairvoyant faculty is fully developed, one sees the Divinity behind the form, the Truth behind the mask. He contemplates Reality and sees the Presence of God everywhere.

Do you blame the Government, external conditions, family, employers, etc., for any problems or limitations you may be experiencing? It is easy to blame others. Are you capable of interpreting that which you see, or do you judge according to appearances? Objective appearance is not always true. Let us call James the Less to discipleship, and let our judgment be as the noon day—noon casts no shadow. I stand on my shadow, therefore, nothing comes in my way to deflect me from judging righteously. No shadow must cross our path—the world of confusion shall lay rejected. Our judgment shall be righteousness, which is wholeness, peace, and perfection.

Thaddeus means of the heart, warm hearted, and praise. Thaddeus represents the exalted mood, the happy, joyous state. *I, if I be lifted up from the earth, will draw all men unto me.* JOHN 12:32. This is the attitude of mind of the man who is disciplining Thaddeus. You lift others up by rejoicing that they are now possessing and expressing all that you long to see them express.

You can praise the flowers in the pot, and they will grow luxuriously and beautifully. Ask the plant to bend over and kiss you; it will. It will grow towards you so that you may kiss it just as a dog will jump on your lap when you indicate you will pet and fondle him.

When you go into a restaurant and the waitress takes a long time to serve you, do you criticize her or suggest that she should be discharged, or do you lift her up in consciousness and see her as she ought to be?

Do you see men as beggars? If this is true, you have clothed them in rags. They are Kings walking the King's Highway! Let us clothe them with the garment of salvation and the robe of righteousness. The beggar will be transformed; he will not be at the street corner tomorrow. This is an example of calling Thaddeus to discipleship.

Praise radiates and gives glory and beauty to the inner powers of man. Let us emulate St. Thaddeus and walk the earth with the praise of God forever on our lips.

Another disciple is Simon of Canaan. Simon means hearing, hearkening. It means one who listens and obeys the voice of the One Who Forever Is. When you discipline this faculty, you look for and expect spiritual guidance and illumination direct from the fountainhead of God. You become still and listen for the still, small voice, the vibration or tone within you that wells up and says, *This is the way, walk ye in.*

Simon of Canaan may be summed up as receptivity to the inner voice of wisdom, truth, and beauty. This leads you to the land of Canaan—the promised land—the realization of harmony, health, and peace. You hear only the good news about ourselves and others; you expect the best. The man who disciplines this faculty of mind lives in a state of joyous expectancy; invariably the best comes to him. The word of God goes before such a man as a pillar of a cloud, to lead them the way; and by night in *a pillar of fire, to give them light; to go by day and night.* EXOD. 13:21.

Do you now gossip, dissect others, criticize them, and indulge in back-biting? These negative qualities would prevent you from controlling and disciplining this important faculty of mind. Do you hear and feel only the best for others? If you can, turn not aside; faint not; the Truth shall lead you to a land of plenty (Canaan) flowing with the milk of life eternal and the honey of unblemished wisdom.

Judas means limitation, the sense of need, desire, or the irredeemed life forces. We are all born with Judas, because we are born into a world where we are conscious of boundaries, time, distance, and other limitations. *Thou has been in Eden, the garden of God; every precious stone was thy covering.* EZEK. 28:13. Yes, we were in a desireless state! Now we are born into a three dimensional world; we have desires. Our failure to realize our desires, cherished hopes, and ideals is the cause of our frustrations and discord. Lack of understanding has caused men to lust, hate, and be greedy for other people's property, territory, possessions, and land; so it is said Judas carried the bag of money (sense of need, limitation). When we discipline this faculty, it is one of the greatest of all the disciples, as it reveals the Truth that sets us free.

We are told Judas betrayed Jesus. If I betray you, I must know your secret; the secret is Christ or Wisdom. Betray means to reveal. Every problem reveals its own solution in the form of a desire. Judas is necessary for the drama; as through our problems we discover the Christ within—the I Am, our own awareness—to be our savior. The joy is in overcoming our problems. When we accept our desire, symbolized by Judas (desire) kissing Jesus (act of love), Judas dies or commits suicide, and the savior (our answered prayer) is revealed or made manifest.

As long as you have the desire, you have not realized it. The moment, however, the desire dies by your acceptance or conviction of your good, a sense of peace steals over you; you are at rest. In the ultimate sense when man dies to all false beliefs, fears, superstitions, racial prejudices, creeds, and color, Christ, which means the Presence of God individualized, is revealed because the distilled essence of man is God; then he is calling forth Mazzaroth. *Canst thou bring forth Mazzaroth?* JOB 38:32. The Judas (sense of limitation and bondage), in you is transformed and redeemed when you die (detachment) to all sense evidence, belief in being of a certain race, age, nationality, etc.

You discipline Judas when you surrender yourself to the influx of Divine Love, and consecrate yourself to a purity of purpose. Divine Love overcomes all problems and transforms the sense man into his pure, original state. The Holy Spirit anoints you; you are resurrected, and the God-man is revealed.

Have you any religious or political prejudices now? Do you like to retain your prejudices? If this is true, you are not disciplining Judas because Judas means detachment which is a divine indifference. Indifference is the tie that severs.

Love is that which binds us to our good, which means that we take our attention away from that which we do not want and focus it on our good or our ideal. Love is wholehearted attention and devotion to the Truth; you must love no other power. You must kill Judas yourself. When you die to all false beliefs, you are back again in the garden of God. *Thou hast been in Eden, the garden of God; every precious stone was thy covering.* EZEK. 28:13.

Yes, truly you are the Christ. *In him there is neither Jew nor Greek, there is neither bond nor free, there is neither male nor female.* GAL. 3:28. You were one with God when the foundation was laid; this foundation is God. The only begotten Son is every man because each man is begotten of the Only One. You must awaken to your true being and discover who you are—sons or expressions of God walking the earth.

You, the reader, represent Jesus and the twelve disciples. As the sun moves through the Zodiac in its cycle, in like manner, symbolically speaking, must your sun (the Holy Spirit) move through your twelve faculties inspiring and breathing into them the Light and Life of He Who Is. As you discipline these faculties as outlined in this book, you consciously become God's radiation dissolving barriers between men.

You must paint the true picture of the ideal man—Jesus the Christ, and not the hideous picture painted over two thousand years ago of a man of sorrows bleeding on the cross with a crown of thorns. Let us tell the youth of the nation the true psychological story of Jesus; then all boys and girls will want to emulate the victor. No boy wants to be the victim. We have been searching for "the lost word" not knowing and not realizing that when it is discovered, it would be in our own manger surrounded by the animals, and marked by a blazing star or burning bush.

The blazing star is I Am. You can find it and become Christed or awakened to your Godhood here and now, and go back to the glory which was yours before the world was. *I have glorified thee on the earths, I have finished the work which thou gavest me to do. And now, O Father; glorify thou me with thine own self with the glory which I had with thee before the world was.* JOHN 17:4–5. Before the world was I Am. Before Abraham was I Am. When all things cease to be, I Am.

33

Comments on Chapter 40, The Book of Job

(3) Then Job answered the Lord, and said, (4) Behold, I am vile; what shall I answer thee? I will lay mine hand upon my mouth.

Job now senses a Presence within his being and is ready now to become still, lay his hand upon his mouth, and give heed to Reality. As Emerson says in one of his essays, "Religion is the emotion of reverence which the presence of the universal mind ever excites in the individual."

The new Job, the illumined man who has awakened to his Indwelling God (Elihu) now comes forth out of the various stages of consciousness depicted in the unfolding of the drama of Job's life from five sense evidence and body consciousness to the new regenerated Job ready to hearken to the voice of Reality. Job now sees the Light and says, "I, the imperfect (as Job), adore my own perfect." Emerson.

(10) *Deck thyself now with majesty and excellency; and array thyself with glory and beauty.* (14) *Then will I also confess unto thee that thine own right hand can save thee.*

These verses point out that you must begin, and then God will respond. We call this the law of action and reaction. When you meet the necessary requirements or establish the proper mental receptivity, then there is always a response from the God Presence within your subliminal depths. God brings something wonderful into your world by working through your thought. He does nothing for you except through you. God has already given you everything. He has created your body, established the world, started your heart beat, and given you a conscious and subconscious mind. He controls all the functions of your body automatically; however, in order for you to advance and grow spiritually you must from this point forward initiate all progress through your own thought.

(15) *Behold now behemoth, which I made with thee, he eateth grass as an ox.*

Some readers go off at a tangent in their interpretation of *behemoth*, and give you a lesson in the natural history of the hippopotamus and his habits. The behemoth is a symbol for unenlightened reasoning based on physical causation. You can build up quite a case for cancer, tuberculosis, and poliomyelitis, and unless you know the Truth you will not be made free from its terrors. Disease is not independent of the mind, and you must awaken to the fact that the germ of cancer is fear which disturbs the mind and the latter condenses down and takes the shape of any idea or mental image given to it.

(19) *He is the chief of the ways of God: he that made him can make his sword to approach unto him. (20) Surely the mountains bring him forth food, where all the beasts of the field play.*

He (reasoning, conscious mind, choice) is the chief of the ways of God in the sense that what you believe governs all your reactions and circumstances. He (behemoth) feeds on mere flesh opinions, suggestions, fears, etc.). You must be armored with the sword of spiritual insight and clarity of thought and destroy all false reasoning based on a suppositional opposing power. The belief or thought of an antagonistic power is a delusion and a snare.

(23) *Behold, he drinketh up a river, and hasteth not: he trusteth that he can draw up Jordan into his mouth. (24) He taketh it with his eyes: his nose pierceth through snares.*

So formidable is behemoth, the symbol of physical matter of fact causation that you must needs be firmly poised in the awareness that the Infinite Power is real only, and all else a lie. Evil seems to work as a power, but really is not a part of Reality. Your belief makes you crawl before the illusion and false beliefs of the world, and you play into the hands of the race mind beliefs.

34

Comments on Chapter 41, The Book of Job

(1) Canst thou draw out leviathan with an hook? or his tongue with a cord which thou lettest down? (2) Canst thou put an hook into his nose? or bore his jaw through with a thorn?

Leviathan, Isaiah's crooked serpent, is a symbol of belief in evil (duality, belief in two powers, or good and evil). Without *behemoth* (reasoning from false premises) leviathan could not exist. Ignorance breeds evil, for if you do not know God within, you must think He must be something outside or up in the skies. Knowing God is your I Amness, awareness and consciousness will melt down mountains of error.

(8) Lay thine hand upon him, remember the battle, do no more.

Do not resist evil. Do not wax angry at evil for this makes it more tenacious. Overcome evil with good or the contemplation of the Presence of God.

(15) *His scales are his pride, shut up together as with a close seal.* (16) *One is so near to another, that no air can come between them.* (17) *They are joined one to another, they stick together, that they cannot be sundered.*

Belief in physical causation is so closely interwoven, so plausible to senses that no air (enlightenment) can come into play unless you are aware of spiritual realities. Only he that made behemoth or leviathan can slay him. It is all a matter of consciousness of God. Right thinking is always miraculous—being the Power of God in man.

(22) *In his neck remaineth strength, and sorrow is turned into joy before him.*

Some people really enjoy bad health, and thank God that they are just a little better. Through the habit of self-pity they succeed in building a martyr complex.

(34) *He beholdeth all high things: he is a king over all the children of pride.*

He (leviathan—sense evidence, race mind beliefs, etc.) is a king over all the children of pride in this way, the sense of evil (sense evidence) is proud of his children (weapons of warfare, armaments, religious persecution, racial prejudice, etc.). The spawning of evil progeny would not be possible if you would recall the One Power and the One Presence within, and feel a deep sense of Its reality.

35

Comments on Chapter 41, The Book of Job

(5) I have heard of thee by the hearing of the ear: but now mine eye seeth thee.

Job is now inwardly perceiving the truth about God. His outer senses cannot see the reason for fear any more, and he no longer fears the threatening voice of the world. The Light of faith in God is dawning in his mind, and he sees the great truths of God in the same way that a boy sees the truth of a chemical equation. Job has a conviction in the goodness and ever availability of the God-Presence at all times and in all emergencies. The Light of the Inner One is dawning in his mind, and he understands and inwardly sees the way God works. Job can now affirm the presence of all things good even though not discernible to the naked eye or the conscious mind. Divine Intelligence is now acting as his Light, and he walks in the faith of freedom, abundance, and peace of mind.

(7) *And it was so, that after the Lord had spoken these words unto Job, the Lord said to Eliphaz the Temanite, My wrath is kindled against thee, and against thy two friends: for ye have not spoken of me the thing that is right, as my servant Job hath. (8) Therefore take unto you now seven bullocks and seven rams, and go to my servant Job, and offer up for yourselves a burnt offering; and my servant Job shall pray for you: for him will I accept: lest I deal with you after your folly, in that ye have not spoken of me the thing which is right, like my servant Job. (9) So Eliphaz the Temanite and Bildad the Shuhite and Zophar the Naamathite went, and did according as the Lord commanded them: the Lord also accepted Job.*

In these verses the whole issue is drawn and the entire mental conflict solved. God approves and finds as his beloved son the new Job and disowns his false friends who spoke from distorted creedal beliefs, misguided influence of race mind beliefs missing the thing that is right, or in other words, telling falsehoods about the nature of God.

In verse eight the essence of the Levitical law of sacrifice is set forth. The illumined reason of the new man is commanded to take all ideals formulated through the five senses plus the creative capacity of the conscious and subconscious mind (conceiving and creating), and make use of these seven senses or creative faculties (symbolized by seven bullocks, rams) in the right way by being aligned mentally with Infinite Power and Boundless Love, thereby consuming and burning up everything unlike God in the mind and body. In order to advance spiritually, we must give up the lesser for the greater. This is symbolized in these verses as the sacrifice of animals.

The sacrifice you make is to give up negative destructive thinking, all negative emotions, and to make a place in your soul (subconscious mind) for the higher qualities of goodness, love, and truth. The sacrifice of animals means the practice of the great law of substitution, such as giving love for hatred, bringing joy where there is sadness, bringing light where there is darkness, and entering into the spirit of forgiveness where ill will is.

Job's senses (Eliphaz), intellect (Bildad), and emotion (Zophar) are redirected and anointed spiritually, and are made ready to enter the Holy of Holies, the heart of the true temple, on the holy mountain. All of which means that you still the wheels of your mind, and you become aware that the Infinite Being is thinking in you, and His thoughts become harmony, peace, joy, ecstasy, and illumination. In the light of this new state of consciousness, philosophy (Eliphaz) is seen as the wisdom of God, theology (Bildad) as the true knowledge of God, and psychology (Zophar) as the soul or place of God bringing peace to the troubled mind.

(10) *And the Lord turned the captivity of Job, when he prayed for his friends: also the Lord gave Job twice as much as he had before.*

Your friends are health, happiness, peace, joy, and all the things that add to your inner security in life. You turn your captivity, or come out of the house of bondage, thralldom, and misery when you claim the qualities, attributes of God as your own, and when you accept mentally all the blessings of heaven. What you affirm and claim as true the Spirit within will honor and objectify in your experience, and you discover that it is God giveth the increase, and He multiplies your good exceedingly. There are many people who suffer from arthritis, rheumatism, asthma and other afflictions, and they discover that when they pray for others similarly affected they have a wonderful healing themselves.

A good way to forget yourself and take your mind off your problems, difficulties, pains, and aches, is to pray for someone else. Do this sincerely and honestly as often as you are led to do so, or until the condition is cleared up. In this procedure you will find your own burden lifted, and the dove of peace will whisper in your ear, "Peace be still."

I have taught a great number of people suffering from acute depression and melancholia to pray for someone in the block, perhaps a person who had a heart attack or a notice of dispossession. I have also encouraged them to visit some friend who is troubled, and try and cheer him up in every way possible through prayer, oral suggestion, and a redirection of interest along constructive lines. Pray for your friends, and wonders will happen as you pray.

(11) *Then came there unto him all his brethren, and all his sisters, and all they that had been of his acquaintance before, and did eat bread with him in his house: and they bemoaned him, and comforted him over all the evil that the Lord had brought upon him: every man also gave him a piece of money, and every one an earring of gold. (12) So the Lord blessed the latter end of Job more than his beginning: for he had fourteen thousand sheep, and six thousand camels, and a thousand yoke of oxen, and a thousand she asses. (13) He had also seven sons and three daughters. (14) And he called the name of the first, Jemima; and the name of the second, Kerzia; and the name of the third Keren-happuch. (15) And in all the land were no women found so fair as the daughters of Job; and their father gave them inheritance among their brethren. (16) After this lived Job an hundred and forty*

years, and saw his sons, and his sons' sons, even four gen-
erations. (17) So Job died, being old and full of days.

These verses depict and portray the transfiguration scene in the life of Job. His seven sons (the regenerated and awakened senses) and the creative powers
of his subjective mind such as desire (Jemima), decision, conception (Kerzia), and manifestation (Keren-
happuch) are all fused into the mystic and magical
rod of right identification with God's eternal verities (transfiguration process) which frees Job from all
limitations and establishes him in his Father's House
again in an advanced self-conscious power pattern
seen only On The Mount or exalted state of consciousness arrived at through communion with God.

Let these great truths of the Book of Job expa-
tiated on in these many chapters be like a sachet of
myrrh, cassia, saffron, and cinnamon carried near
your heart enabling you to release from the treasure
house of eternity the sweet fragrance and perfume of
Divinity now and forevermore.

About the Author

A native of Ireland who resettled in America, Joseph Murphy, Ph.D., D.D. (1898–1981) was a prolific and widely admired New Thought minister and writer, best known for his metaphysical classic, *The Power of Your Subconscious Mind*, an international bestseller since it first appeared on the self-help scene in 1963. A popular speaker, Murphy lectured on both American coasts and in Europe, Asia, and South Africa. His many books and pamphlets on the auto-suggestive and metaphysical faculties of the human mind have entered multiple editions—some of the most poignant of which appear in this volume. Murphy is considered one of the pioneering voices of affirmative-thinking philosophy.